D1217092

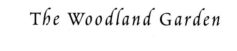

The Woodland Garden

THE WOODLAND GARDEN

ROBERT GILLMORE

Photographs and Illustrations by Eileen Oktavec

Taylor Publishing Company
Dallas, Texas

Also by Robert Gillmore

Great Walks of Acadia National Park & Mount Desert
Great Walks of Southern Arizona
Great Walks of Big Bend National Park
Great Walks of the Great Smokies
Great Walks of Yosemite National Park
Great Walks of Sequoia & Kings Canyon National Parks
Great Walks of Acadia National Park & Mount Desert Island, revised edition
Liberalism and the Politics of Plunder: The Conscience of a Neo-Liberal

Copyright 1996 by Robert Gillmore

Published by Taylor Publishing
1550 West Mockingbird Lane
Dallas, TX 75235

Designed by Hespenheide Design

Library of Congress Cataloging–in–Publication Data

Gillmore, Robert.
      The woodland garden/Robert Gillmore: photographs
and illustrations by Eileen Oktavec.
          p. cm.
      Includes index.
      ISBN 0-87833-924-8
      1. Woodland gardening. 2. Low maintenance gardening.
3. Gardens—United States. 4. Gardens—Canada. I. Okatvec,
Eileen. II. Title.
SB439.6.G54 1995
635.9'76—dc20   95-40155
                                                  CIP

Printed in the United States of America
10 9 8 7 6 5 4 3 2 1

To Eileen

CONTENTS

ACKNOWLEDGMENTS

One of the greatest pleasures of writing this book has been meeting people who've shared my enthusiasm for gardens in general and for this project in particular and who've helped me in many ways.

I want to thank Timothy Taylor of the Asticou Terraces (and Thuja Garden) and Mary Roper of the Asticou Azalea Garden, both in Northwest Harbor, Maine; Cheryl Lowe of the Garden in the Woods in Framingham, Massachusetts; Neal Calvanese and Marianne Cramer of Central Park in New York City; Denise Mangani, Linda Eirhart, Hillary Holland, and their colleagues at Winterthur, Delaware; Colvin Randall, Jeff Lynch, and Larry Albee of Longwood Gardens in Pennsylvania; W. Gary Smith, ASLA, designer of the refurbished Peirce's Woods at Longwood; Richard Lighty of Mt. Cuba Center for the Study of Piedmont Flora in Greenville, Delaware; Anita Bailiff and Joe Kosh at Airlie Gardens in Wilmington, North Carolina; Donna Cox of Middleton Place in South Carolina; Pat Collins, Sonia Eakins, and Angie Moody of Callaway Gardens in Pine Mountain, Georgia; Beth Weidner of Maclay State Gardens in Tallahassee, Florida; Charlene Johnson of Bok Tower Gardens in Lake Wales, Florida; Mary Moats and Len Musick of Hodges Gardens in Many, Louisiana; Karen Pardick and Jim Jackson of Descanso Gardens in La Canada Flintridge, California; Scott Gregory Vergara and his staff at the Rhododendron Species Garden in Federal Way, Washington; Tony Toste, Nancy Swanson, and Gregory Dyment at Lakewold Gardens in Tacoma, Washington; Richard Brown and Patricia Ostenson of the Bloedel Reserve on Bainbridge Island, Washington; Kristi O'Donnell of the Meerkerk Rhododendron Garden in Greenbank, Washington; Daniel Zatz and Michael Boswell of the Miller Garden in Seattle, Washington; Linda Blaine, Junji Shinada, and Mildred Greggor of the Nitobe Memorial Garden at the University of British Columbia

Botanical Garden in Vancouver, Canada; Mike and Vickie Short at the Ohme Gardens in Wenatchee, Washington; Ted Van Veen of the Crystal Springs Rhododendron Garden in Portland, Oregon; and Michael Robert of Hendricks Park Rhodendron Garden in Eugene, Oregon.

I am also grateful to my agent, Robin Straus; to my editor, Macy Jaggers; and to my secretary, Claire Baker, who proofread the manuscript. Their diligence, remarkable abilities, and unflagging enthusiasm made my life easier and this book better than either would have been without their efforts.

I am most grateful, however, to my fiancée, Eileen Oktavec, an accomplished artist, photographer, writer, gardener, and landscape designer in her own right. Eileen drew all the illustrations and took almost all the photographs in this book, and her criticisms have been of enormous benefit to both my writing and my gardens.

Robert Gillmore
Evergreen
Goffstown, New Hampshire
December 1995

TEN REASONS FOR A WOODLAND GARDEN

Do you recognize this picture? It's a house surrounded by shrubs, flower beds, a large lawn, and woods. The shrubs, flower beds, and lawn are all carefully weeded, watered, raked, and clipped. The woodland, however, is mostly ignored—it's left growing wild. As Hamlet said about the world, it's "an unweeded garden, . . . things rank and gross in nature / Possess it merely."

And that's a shame. For instead of an unweeded woodland—one where dead branches lie wherever they fall and anything is allowed to grow wherever it wants—our woods, with relatively little effort, could be woodland gardens composed of large, spreading trees, handsome evergreen shrubs, and shade-loving ground covers and flowers.

One irony is that, instead of being the least attractive parts of our land, woodlands can actually be one of the most beautiful—

and for only a fraction of the time and money we spend on our lawns and flowers.

A woodland garden has ten distinct advantages over lawns and flower beds.

1. AN EXTRA DIMENSION
A well-designed garden is like a room: it has a floor, walls, and a ceiling. The floor usually includes grass, ground covers, flowers, and other low plants. The walls are typically large shrubs, trees, fences, etc.; and the ceiling is usually the canopy formed by the overhanging branches of large trees.

The gardens around most homes have well-made floors but weak or even nonexistent walls and ceilings. That's because plants in these gardens—the lawn and flowers—grow on or close to the ground, and the trees are far too few to create a wall, let alone a ceiling.

A woodland garden, on the other hand, has many trees. They are its essence. They give the garden its walls and ceiling—its extra dimension. Most gardens have only two dimensions—the length and width of the landscape floor. Woodland gardens have three: length, width, and the height provided by the trees. In most gardens, the plants are mainly below you; you walk almost entirely over beauty. In a woodland garden, the plants are above, below, and all around you. Instead of walking over them, you are enveloped by them. Instead of walking over beauty, you walk, as Lord Byron put it, *in* beauty. Or, in the words of the Navajo prayer, "With beauty before me . . . beauty behind me . . . beauty above me . . . beauty below me . . . beauty all around me."

2. A COMPLETE LANDSCAPE

Because a woodland garden fills the entire landscape—the length, width, and height of the outdoor room—it can fulfill the first principle of design, which is unity.

Like any work of art—in fact, like anything of beauty—a garden must be whole. In a landscape, the whole is simply everything you can see. If you can see it from your garden, it's *in* your garden. And if it's *in* your garden, it must be visually related—it must be in harmony with everything else you can see—or you've got to get it out of your garden. If you can't use it, you've got to lose it.

Many home gardens lack unity because too many things that should be out of the garden aren't. A house may have lush foundation shrubs, a dazzling green lawn, and colorful flowers but they don't go with—in fact, they have absolutely nothing to do with—the blue vinyl siding on one neighbor's house, the silver-colored storm windows on another, the bicycles on the concrete sidewalk, the cars and trucks on the asphalt street or the telephone poles and electric wires stretching in every direction. There are some beautiful things in the landscape, but the whole landscape is a mess.

A woman who lived in a handsome house on a street with other handsome houses once offered to show me her garden. She took me to a bed of well-tended perennials that ran between the edge of her property and her neighbor's driveway. I looked down at the flowers. Then I looked at a truck parked in the street.

"How do you like the truck in your garden?" I asked.

"I beg your pardon?" she answered.

Then the truck drove away.

"Never mind," I said, "it's not in your garden any more."

Unfortunately, from where we stood, I could see eight houses, five telephone poles, two streets, several driveways, and four cars. They were in her garden, and most would not be leaving anytime soon.

A woodland garden is a different kind of garden. If they're large enough, the tree-made walls of its outdoor rooms will screen out houses, cars, roads, utility poles, and all the other impedimenta of civilization. In their place will be a whole landscape. A landscape to which, as Aristotle said of a work of art, nothing needs to be added and nothing needs to be taken away.

3. A LITTLE WORLD OF NATURE
A woodland garden, however, doesn't remove only the inharmonious aspects of our civilization. It also removes almost every trace of our manmade world. The woodland garden realizes the most precious promise of any garden, which is to create a little world of nature within the larger world of civilization.

Most home gardens don't even pretend to fulfill this promise. They're too small and two-dimensional. The lawns beside our streets and the shrubs beside our houses don't take us away from civilization. Instead of being a respite from our man-made world, they're ornaments in that world.

A woodland garden, on the other hand, does not decorate our manmade world. It bids it goodbye. Instead of houses decorated with nature, the woodland garden offers simply Nature itself.

4. IDEALIZED NATURE
The woodland garden is more beautiful than a wild, unweeded woodland because it is, after all, a garden. Like any garden, it's tidied up, graded, weeded, planted, and pruned. In a woodland garden, as in all gardens, nature is edited. What should be taken away is taken away. What should be added is added. The result is idealized nature: a garden that looks natural—that looks as if it *could* have been made by nature—but actually looks better than most woodlands made by nature alone.

5. IT'S ALREADY THERE
Unlike lawns and flower gardens, a woodland garden isn't made from scratch. Part of it is already there. And not just any part but its biggest part: trees. And not just any trees, but big, old, mature trees that are unavailable in any nursery at any price—and, if they were, would cost literally thousands of dollars. All these trees—in some gardens literally tens of thousands of dollars' worth of landscape stock—are yours for the using. Robert Frost called them "a gift outright."

Better still, they're already planted. There's no need to hire a tree spade the size of a dump truck for $130 an hour; no need to dig room-size holes; no need to tie, feed, water, and worry. And no need to wait until they grow. The biggest, most expensive, most essential part of your garden is already there.

"Gee, I wish I had a nice garden," someone once said to me. I looked at the neglected grove of large white pines (*Pinus strobus*) behind her house and at the luxurious brown carpet of needles beneath.

I pointed to the pines and replied, "You already have a nice garden. It just needs a little work."

Often your legacy will include more than trees. One client of mine had purchased a new house on a three-acre lot and asked me to help him landscape it. In the woods behind his house was half an acre of mountain laurel (*Kalmia latifolia*), known for its exquisite white blossoms. The six-foot-high shrubs almost covered the ground.

"Not much to do here," I said. "Just take out the dead wood, build some paths, cut some trees to let in more light so the laurel will bloom better, and you'll have an extraordinary laurel grove."

Still other woods may already have rhododendrons or other evergreen shrubs, or perhaps myrtle (*Vinca minor*), pachysandra, or other ground covers, or Solomon's-seal (*Polygonatum biflorum*), lily-of-the-valley (*Convallaria majalis*), or other attractive wildflowers—not to mention brooks, ponds, and handsome rocks and rock formations. Few other landscapes will already be so much like a garden as a woodland.

6. IT COSTS LESS THAN LESSER GARDENS

Another irony of a woodland garden is that this rich, tree-studded landscape—with more plant mass than any other garden—can be yours for only a fraction of the time and money required by grass and flower beds. The typical lawn-and-flower garden needs planting, seeding, reseeding, watering, mulching, fertilizing, mowing, weeding, and raking forever. Woodland gardens need virtually none of these things. They don't need mowing because they have no turf. They need little if any raking, mulching, or fertilizing because their leaves, needles, and other debris remain where they fall and mulch and fertilize the soil naturally. Woodland gardens don't need seeding, reseeding, or replanting because their plants are trees, shrubs, perennials, or naturally reseeding annuals and biennials. They need little watering because they're kept cool and moist by their own natural leaf-and-needle mulch and shady tree canopy, and because their plants get most if not all of the water they need from rain and snow. Woodland gardens need little weeding because their natural mulch and shade canopy inhibit other plants. Once installed, a properly designed woodland garden needs only seasonal cleanup (mainly of dead trees and branches), occasional watering, just a little weeding, and even less pruning. That's why a woodland garden costs almost nothing to maintain. A woodland garden costs more money and time to create than a lawn or flower bed, but in the long run it costs less than either one.

7. A CAPITAL INVESTMENT

Like a forest, a woodland garden largely takes care of itself. A lawn and especially a flower garden are different. Left alone, they're consumable goods: they wear out. If they do survive they do so only with constant maintenance.

What's more, a woodland garden doesn't merely survive with little care. It flourishes. Within just a few years of planting, a woodland garden's shrubs, perennials, and ground covers grow full and lush. And they'll keep growing year after year. Grass and flowers, on the other hand, require hours of care just to endure.

The woodland garden is not just a capital improvement, it's a capital invest-ment. It actually grows in size and value year after year. Left alone, lawn or flower gardens steadily depreciate. With constant care they only maintain, never increase, their value. How could they? Unlike the trees and shrubs of a woodland garden, they don't get bigger.

8. SAVING ENERGY

If it's close enough to your house, a wood-land garden can help keep it cooler in the summer and warmer in the winter.

Deciduous trees provide summer cool-ing and winter heating automatically. When their leaves are out in the summer, they shade your house, reducing and sometimes even eliminating air-conditioning costs. In the winter, when deciduous trees are bare, they let the sun shine on your house. This extra sunshine makes your house warmer and reduces the cost of heating your home. Evergreen trees can also reduce your heat-ing costs. By sheltering your home from strong winter winds, they reduce both heat loss and cold-air infiltration.

Every tree helps cool the air around your house—and therefore the house itself—by transpiring water vapor through its needles or leaves. Large trees transpire thousands of gallons of water a day. Luckily for us, most transpiration occurs in the summer, when trees are most active and when we need their cooling effect the most.

9. GOOD FOR THE ENVIRONMENT

Trees are good for the environment, and a woodland garden has more trees than any other kind of garden. By reducing the energy needed to heat and cool our houses, trees make it possible for us to burn less fossil fuel, thereby reducing air pollution. Trees are also natural air filters: they reduce the danger of global warming by removing carbon dioxide from the air.

10. IT'S COMFORTABLE

Woodland gardens are, literally, the coolest gardens of all. That's partly because they're shadier than any other kind of garden. The shade keeps the hot sun not only off us but also off most of the garden, helping it stay moist and cool. It's also kept cool by the water vapor transpired by trees.

A woodland garden will be cool—or at least the coolest place on your property—on a warm day, and it'll be a shady spot on any day. On many hot, sunny days a woodland garden may be the most pleasant place to be in the entire yard—a lush, serene oasis, a refreshing island of relief from the torrid temperatures of summer.

When your woodland garden is complete, it will have one or more outdoor rooms. On the floor of the rooms will be paths. Beside the paths will be low, shade-loving plants—mostly evergreen ground covers, some perennial flowers, and a few annuals for summer-long color. Behind the low plants and farther away from the paths will be taller, mainly evergreen shrubs. Still farther away will be the trees—the walls and ceilings of the outdoor rooms.

Creating those beautiful rooms is among the most exciting, most satisfying gardening you can do. And it isn't difficult. All you have to do is follow the steps outlined in this book.

You don't have to begin all these steps immediately. Woodland gardening isn't an all-or-nothing proposition. If, for example, your budget is tight and you can't afford many shrubs or other plants, you can postpone planting and concentrate on cleaning up, weeding, and pruning. Those steps will dramatically improve the appearance of your woods all by themselves. What's more, if you do the work yourself, it will cost you virtually nothing. (And you'll get some free exercise, too.)

After I explain the six steps to making a woodland garden, I'll describe how easy it is to maintain your woodland garden after it's finished.

To show you how these steps were used to create an actual garden, I'll describe how I used them to transform a white pine forest into my own .8-acre woodland garden, appropriately named Evergreen.

To show you how beautiful woodland gardens can be, I will also describe and illustrate some of North America's best examples, including the spruce-covered Asticou Terraces in Northeast Harbor, Maine; the azalea woodlands of the South; and the evergreen-shaded rhododendron gardens of the Pacific Northwest. Every one of these gardens is open to the public, so you can enjoy and study them firsthand. I also list several public arboretums and botanical gardens where you can get a close look at shade-tolerant shrubs, ground covers, and perennials suitable for a woodland garden.

PART ONE

CREATING

A WOODLAND

GARDEN

SETTING PRIORITIES—DECIDING
WHAT AND WHERE TO GARDEN FIRST

Woodland gardens are usually larger than other kinds of gardens for two reasons.

First, woodland gardens are at their best when the sights and sounds of civilization are excluded and the garden can be a purely natural space. To exclude civilization, gardens need depth: they must be large enough to have a buffer of earth, rocks, trees, etc. that is thick enough to block views of neighbors' houses, the sounds of traffic, and other evidence of the manmade world. The closer the garden is to the non-natural world, the thicker the buffer must be.

Second, woodland gardens are larger than other gardens simply because they include at least a few trees, and a few trees take up more room than, say, an equal number of shrubs. Just a half dozen large trees, for example, may spread across several hundred square feet.

Because woodland gardens tend to be relatively large, you probably won't have time and money to turn all of your woods into a garden immediately. Instead you'll want to set priorities: you must decide what parts of your woods you want to garden first.

Which ones?

That's simple: the parts you already see and the parts you want to see. Here are some examples:

- Places you see from windows and other vantage points *inside* your house.
- Places you see from *outside* your house—from decks or porches; from your lawn or other parts of the yard where you walk.
- Sections of the woods where you walk or would like to walk, such as:

- Near interesting or beautiful features like streams, waterfalls, ponds, large rocks, ledges, cliffs, and viewpoints.
- Beside beautiful or interesting trees, shrubs, ground covers, flowers, and other plants already growing on your property.
- Places where trees, rocks, or other features already create a sense of enclosure—incipient outdoor rooms.
- Low sites that would be appropriate for artificial ponds—especially if you don't have natural bodies of water already in place.
- Clearings that would be perfect for sunny gardens deep in the woods.
- Areas you need to walk through to get to the places listed above.

If you don't already know what portions of your woods you can see from your house or yard, take a look out your windows and, if you need to, mark the boundaries of the vistas with stakes.

If you don't already know the special features of your woods, find out. Walk every part of your woodland. Go slowly and carefully. Take time to look at everything. Make this trip often, at least once in the spring, several times in the summer, and a couple of times in the early fall. That way you'll see your woodland in all its phases. You'll see shrubs that bloom only in the spring; flowers that blossom only in June, July, or August; and trees that turn color only in the fall. If you plan to enjoy your woodland garden in the winter, walk your woods then too—especially to discover the trees (such as beeches and many oaks) that keep many of their leaves through the winter. Only by walking your woods in every season will you discover all its assets. The more trips you make, the more you'll learn and the better you'll be able to decide which plants should be removed and which should be saved.

When you learn where all the special features of your woods are, you'll also be able to figure out the best ways to get to them. This interesting task is called path-making, explained later.

All things equal, the places in your woods most worthy of gardening (other than those near your house) are usually near the center of the woodland. The center is usually farthest away from roads, neighbors' houses, and other development around your house, where the sights and sounds of civilization are least apt to intrude and where the woodland garden can reach its fullest potential as a totally natural garden.

On the other hand, you may not want to garden the sections near streets and houses.

And if the woods here are not thick enough to hide neighboring houses, you may want to build berms to screen them. Berms are explained in Step Three.

THE NATURAL LEGACY OF EVERGREEN

It took me only a short walk around my property to discover that I was the owner of a magnificent natural legacy, one just waiting to be transformed into an extraordinary woodland garden.

For one thing, there were the trees—a forest of large, handsome white pines all around the house. (And my neighbors' houses, too.) Dozens of large, straight, dark brown trunks and a carpet of warm brown needles gave the woods a striking unity. There are few forests quite so lovely as mature pine woods—and I had one!

Then there were the rocks: dozens of gray granite "glacial erratics," so called because they were strewn across the land by a glacier in the last Ice Age. Most of the rocks are of substantial size; some are as large as a Volkswagen Beetle and at least a couple are as big as small cabins. Virtually every one of them is a handsome piece of natural sculpture.

Then there was the exciting shape of the land itself. Many lots are as flat as air-ports. Evergreen, my garden, is a hillside that slopes from north to south and west to east in a series of irregular natural terraces.

At the bottom of the eastern slope, near the eastern edge of the garden, is a seasonal brook lined with dozens of large moss-covered rocks. Because the stream bed slopes steeply from north to south, the brook creates countless small cascades as it rushes downhill. Below the cascades is a shallow pool ringed with moss-covered boulders. Rising steeply up from the east side of the brook are gray granite cliffs, some almost vertical, some nearly twenty feet high.

Another rock feature, on the other side of the property, is a cluster of huge glacial erratics that looks like the opening of a small cave.

One more valued legacy of the property is its plants. Besides the pines, there are smaller oak (*Quercus* spp.), maple (*Acer* spp.), sassafras (*Sassafras albidum*), and witch hazel (*Hamamelis virginiana*) trees. There are also large clusters of hay-scented ferns (*Dennstaedtia punctilobula*), one the size of a large room. In the spring, much of the floor of the woods is carpeted with bright green Canadian mayflower (*Maianthemum canadense*), also known as false lily-of-the-valley. I also found several other interesting herbaceous wildflowers, including pink lady's-slipper orchids (*Cypripedium acaule*); Jack-in-the-pulpit (*Arisaema triphyllum*), named for the leafy hood that hangs over its seed cluster like the top of an old-fashioned pulpit; Solomon's-seal, distinguished by its graceful leaning fronds, long leaves growing perpendicular to their stalks, and tiny, white bell-shaped flowers hanging below the plant; and the similar but larger false Solomon's-seal (*Smilacina racemosa*). Along the stream are patches of forget-me-nots (*Myosotis sylvatica*), revered for their dainty blue-and-white flowers, and several robust European or common barberry bushes (*Berberis vulgaris*), whose leaves and berries turn red in the fall.

Altogether, the natural legacy of Evergreen was literally priceless. Many of its smaller trees and wildflowers could have been bought in a nursery, but its big trees, rocks, cliffs, and stream were not available anywhere at any price. Because they were here, the largest and most elaborate parts of my garden were already complete. Most of Evergreen, in other words, was already built. All I had to do was finish it.

The pines, the rocks, and the shape of the land became what gardeners call "the bones," the major organizing elements of the garden. They helped determine where my paths, plantings, and several outdoor

"rooms" would go. The larger rocks, in fact, helped form some of the rooms. The pines, the cliffs, the cavelike rock cluster, the brook, the pool, and most of the other rocks scattered about the property became some of the most impressive features of the site (as you'll soon see).

Many of the deciduous trees were left to add variety and interest, to provide beautiful fall foliage, and to help screen views of nearby homes. Some witch hazels were pruned to frame views of the cliffs and to create beautiful specimen trees. Most of the attractive wildflowers, including the ferns, were left to provide variety and interesting seasonal accents. Some of the larger patches of fern became major plant groupings.

I also discovered, as I toured the property, that there were many much less attractive smaller trees and shrubs on the site. These had to be pruned or removed entirely. Many smaller rocks had to go, too, as did several decades' worth of dead trees and branches. (These projects are explained in Step Two).

I also made berms to screen the property from surrounding houses and to create several rooms, and I built a quarter-mile of paths to display the garden's features. I installed two fishponds and built two causeways over the seasonal brook. I planted the garden with large drifts of shade-tolerant evergreen shrubs and ground covers and annual and perennial flowers and added furniture and sculpture for utility and low-maintenance color and interest.

My lot is almost an acre in size. I had neither time nor money enough to make it all a garden at once. So I did it gradually, starting with what I saw every day: the 100- to 150-foot band of woodlands immediately around my house. This included both the west side of the lot along the street and the northwest and southwest sections of the property. When these were done, I worked on sections to the east. After about seven years' work, Evergreen was finished.

GARDENING BY SUBTRACTION— CLEANING UP, WEEDING, AND PRUNING

M ost gardening consists mainly of adding shrubs, flowers, and other plants to the garden. Woodland gardening is different. It involves not just adding things to your garden but taking things away as well. I call this "gardening by subtraction."

Michelangelo wrote that a sculpture already exists in the stone—the sculptor merely reveals it by chipping away the stone around it. Similarly, much of a woodland garden already exists in your woods. You have to reveal it by removing some of the plants covering it up. Gardening by subtraction includes cleaning up, weeding, and pruning your woods.

CLEANING UP

Cleanup consists of simply removing all dead wood, both standing and fallen (including diseased and dying trees), as well as all litter and other manmade debris from the site.

Manmade material must be removed not only for the obvious reason—it's usually unsightly trash and other junk—but also because a woodland garden is mainly a natural place in which only a few manmade objects, such as sculpture or furniture, should be allowed to intrude.

Some of the natural material you'll remove will include small stones and other rocks that detract from, rather than add to, the beauty of the garden.

Most of the debris you'll have to remove, however, will be dead trees and branches. Occasionally—only occasionally—a large dead log or stump, especially if it's overgrown with a vine or other plant, is picturesque. But most fallen trees and branches are far from picturesque. On the contrary, they break the woodland landscape's unity that is created in part by the vertical lines of dozens of large tree trunks. Fallen trees and branches must be removed not only because they're clutter but also because their horizontal—or, worse, crooked or diagonal—position clashes with the otherwise consistent verticality of the tree trunks.

TREE REMOVAL Dead trees that are still standing must be removed, too. You may be tempted to leave dead standing trees in place because they're too much trouble to remove and, at least at the moment, they're not objectionable—they're still vertical, so they don't break the unity of the forest, and their bark hasn't fallen off to create unsightly blotches of lighter colored wood on the trunks where bark used to be.

The temptation to leave these trees alone should be resisted. All dead trees lose their bark or topple over within a few years after they die. When they fall they usually do at least some damage to any surrounding trees, shrubs, and flowers.

What's more, you may do even more damage to the surrounding plants when you finally remove the tree.

So the best time to remove all dead trees—fallen and standing—is before you plant the garden. (In fact, the best time to remove anything from the garden is before planting.)

Cleaning up your woods accomplishes two things.

First, a clean woodland looks better—more like a garden—all by itself. After you've removed all the dead trunks and branches you'll notice that your woods are neater, more open, more parklike, more pleasing—all without planting a single shrub! That's why cleaning up isn't, technically, something you do before you make the woodland garden. It's an essential part of woodland gardening.

Second, by removing a lot of the woody clutter, you get a clearer look at your woods, making it easier for you to decide what live trees and other plants you need to weed from the garden and what plants you want to add.

Happily, cleaning up costs almost nothing. If you do the work yourself, the only things you'll have to pay for (if you don't already own them) are some tools: a chain saw or bow saw, a wheelbarrow or garden cart to help carry away the debris, and some work gloves.

Another nice thing about cleaning up is that it's the simplest part of woodland gardening. Most of what you need to know about it can be said in seven words: *If it's dead, get rid of it.*

Identifying dead wood on the ground is easy. Identifying standing dead wood is only slightly more difficult. Trees that have been dead for several years are usually easy to spot because many of their branches and at least some of their bark have fallen off. If the tree is deciduous, it will have no leaves during the growing season; if the tree is a typical evergreen, it will have no green needles.

If you're not sure a tree is dead, look at it carefully, all the way up to the top. If you can't see any leaves or green needles, and if the other trees in the woods do have leaves or needles, you can safely conclude the tree is dead.

When possible, remove the roots of the tree as well as the trunk. If you get rid of the entire tree, you won't have an ugly stump to deal with, and the roots won't be in the way when you plant.

If it's small enough, try to pull the dead tree out of the ground, roots and all. The longer the tree has been dead, the weaker its roots will be, and the more likely you'll be able to yank it out. If you can't pull it up, try toppling it over. (Sometimes it helps to rock it back and forth first.) If you're lucky, the tree will fall over and the roots will come out of the ground with it.

There are three ways to make this work easier:

- ✆ Get help. You'll be pleasantly surprised to discover how big a dead tree three or four people can dislodge! Make sure, of course, that no one is in the way when it falls.
- ✆ Use a come-along, a kind of winch with a steel cable wrapped around

it. You attach one end of the cable to the dead tree and the other end to a much heavier or stable object, such as a large tree, rock, vehicle, etc. Then you move the winch handle back and forth to tighten the cable. If it's not too big, the dead tree will "come along" out of the ground. (You can also attach both ends of the cable to dead trees. If you're lucky, and both of them are about the same size, both of them may come out of the ground.) If you buy or rent a come-along, make sure it's powerful enough to do what you want it to do. Use a leather or heavy cloth strap to attach the cable to a live tree, so you don't scar it.

- ✆ If heavy equipment can reach the site, you can pull trees out with a tractor or other vehicle. Even a garden tractor can remove small trees. Remember that power equipment of any kind can be dangerous. Make sure you learn how to operate it properly before you use it. The company that sells or rents you the equipment can tell you how to use it correctly.

If you can't pull or push the tree out of the ground, you'll have to cut it. Make the cut as close to the ground as possible, so you'll be able to hide the stump by covering it with the smallest possible amount of earth.

WEEDING

Weeding is more complicated than cleanup. In cleaning up, all you have to do is find dead wood—any dead wood—and get rid of it. When you weed, you have to decide which trees, shrubs, and other plants to remove. You have to decide which enhance your garden and which detract from it, and take out the latter.

Exactly which plants you remove will depend, of course, on what you have and where they're growing. In general, however, a few rules of thumb usually apply.

All things equal, the closer a plant is to an extreme size, the more valuable it is. Large trees, particularly evergreens, should almost always be left alone. Small deciduous trees, on the other hand, should almost always be removed. The value of hardwood trees is almost always proportional to their size: the larger the tree, the more likely it is that it should be left alone. The smaller the tree, the more likely it is that it should be taken down.

Why are big trees welcome and small deciduous ones not? That short question has a rather long answer.

A typical residential woodland in the continental United States is a mixture of many deciduous and a few evergreen trees. (Pure evergreen forests usually grow only at higher altitudes or higher latitudes—higher than most residential areas.) The largest trees were probably cut for lumber not long ago, so the stand is usually young. It'll typically have few, if any, really big trees. Instead there will usually be a small number of medium-sized trees and many tall, one- to three-inch-thick saplings, some as skinny as broom handles. Beneath the trees will be a few bushes (especially in sunnier spots) and a number of wildflowers and other small deciduous plants.

The large trees should be left undisturbed for several reasons:

- Their canopy forms the ceiling and their large trunks form the walls of the woodland garden room.
- The large trunks are important organizing elements—the "bones" of the garden.
- Large trees have a presence smaller trees lack. The paradox is this: even though trees are the biggest things in the forest, at eye level they're usually narrower than the smallest shrub. In the woods, a tree trunk must be at least a foot around before it's big enough to have a presence. Unlike large trees, small, skinny saplings are meaningless lines in the landscape, often adding only clutter to the garden.

These saplings are spindly because, in a mature forest, sunlight doesn't penetrate the canopy that forms the ceiling of the woodland room. As a result, the woods are so shady that little trees have barely enough sunlight to survive, let alone flourish. Large trees prosper because they're the tallest things in the woods; there's nothing between their crowns and sunlight. The cruel irony of the forest is that the very canopy that captures life-giving light for big trees creates only deadly shade for small ones.

Sun shines through the tree canopy that forms the ceiling of Evergreen.

A landscape filled with all different sizes of tree stems—small, medium, and large—is hopelessly confused and messy. The trunks of large hardwoods can create one of the most powerfully unified landscapes in the world—the unity of the woodland garden. But they achieve that unity only when they're not crowded by smaller trees. When dozens of small stems with dozens of different diameters share their space, unity is destroyed. Instead of the simple, almost parklike beauty of the woodland garden, you have the messy clutter of the unweeded garden.

Another compelling reason for removing smaller deciduous trees is that the remaining, larger trees will have less competition for water and nutrients, so they'll grow faster and become even more impressive. Ideally, at least a few of these trees will grow to become massive specimens, some of the most treasured focal points in the garden.

This leads me to another rule of thumb: any hardwood smaller than roughly six inches in diameter should probably be removed.

Like all rules, however, this one has exceptions:

- If all the trees on your lot are less than six inches thick, you obviously can't cut them all down and still have a woodland garden. If all your trees are small, leave just enough of the largest to preserve the site as woodland. Remove the rest. (The silver lining on this cloud is that, with the small trees gone, those remaining will get most of the sunlight, water, and nutrients available and grow faster than they would have otherwise.)

- If small trees form a large cluster or clump of the same species, you might want to leave the entire cluster alone—especially if their leaves provide a lot of fall or winter color. Ironically, the smaller the trees in the clump, the more likely they should be left alone. The smaller the tree, the less it's noticed and the less, therefore, it offends. The tree is important not in itself but only as part of the cluster. It should remain because, the more trees in the cluster, the stronger its visual effect.
- Other small trees that should usually be preserved are showy dogwoods (*Cornus* spp.) and other flowering species, and trees with colorful bark, such as white and gray birches (*Betula* spp.). Instead of being cut down, these beauties should get special care (see pruning). Use them as accent plants to provide valuable, low-maintenance color in a garden dominated by greens and browns.
- Small evergreen trees should often be spared, too. Like dogwoods and birches, use them as accents. Like evergreen shrubs, evergreen trees

provide precious year-round green foliage in an otherwise somber early spring or late autumn hardwood forest of brown-barked trees, brown earth paths, and dead brown leaves. Although even shade-tolerant species like hemlocks (*Tsuga* spp.) may not get enough sunlight to grow quickly, the size of the tree doesn't matter. (Shrubs, after all, are small.) What matters is that the tree is full and well shaped.

There are also circumstances when you should remove trees larger than six inches thick:

- Remove any tree if it's unsightly or in an inconvenient location or, for whatever reason, is more of a liability in the garden than an asset.
- Remove trees larger than six inches thick if you want to allow more sunlight into the woods and there are no (or no more) smaller trees available to cut.

ADMITTING SUNLIGHT TO THE GARDEN How much sunlight you want in your garden depends on your goals.

On the one hand, the more light you have, the more varieties of shrubs and flowers you can grow, the fuller the plants will become, and the more blossoms they'll produce.

On the other hand, the more trees you remove to let in more light, the less the site looks like a woodland garden and the more it looks like any other garden. With fewer trees, the garden will be more open and less intimate. The essence of a woodland garden—its wonderful sense of three-dimensional enclosure—is diminished. The garden may also be more exposed to houses and other development around it. What's more, it'll be warmer and drier—it won't be quite as cool and shady on hot, sunny days, you'll have to water and weed more often, and you may have to mulch and fertilize artificially.

Try to leave just the right number of trees to create just the right amount of sunlight—not too little, not too much.

The amount of sunlight doesn't have to be the same throughout the garden. On the contrary, differences are welcome. Deeply shaded areas can be broken up by sunnier ones, including large, sunny clearings.

Whenever you cut trees to admit more sunlight, remember several rules:

- Let in just enough light to make rhododendrons and other flowering shrubs bloom well (about four hours of direct sun a day).
- Let the canopy cover roughly two-thirds of the "ceiling" of the room, leaving about one-third open to the sky. This gives many plants on the garden floor a few hours of daily sunlight—enough for many shade-loving plants to bloom, while leaving enough trees to create a cool, shady, enclosed woodland garden.
- Remove trees in order of their size, starting with the smallest, going to the next larger, then the next larger, until you remove enough trees to admit the amount of light you want.
- Create sunny spots where the trees are already smaller and more sparse than elsewhere in the woods.

Keep these rules in mind and you'll usually get away with cutting fewer trees—and fewer large trees—to let in the same amount of sunlight. In many woodlands, you'll be able to create sunny places simply by removing only small trees.

Another reason the size of a large tree is often more important than its species is that, in many woodlands, the crown of a large tree is so high its leaves are not very noticeable. What's important is what is noticed: the trunk. The particular color or texture of the trunk (i.e., what kind of a tree it is) is usually not significant because the dark brown bark of one tree is usually not appreciably more interesting or attractive than the dark brown bark of another (most trees, after all, are not white birches (*Betula pendula*). What is important about the trunk is usually its size. The bigger the trunk, the more impressive the tree. And the more valuable it is in the garden.

Of course, if you have two or more equally large trees and you have to remove one or more of them, then you can take species and other differences into account. If one tree has a better shape or prettier bark than another, you should probably cut down the less attractive one. But you should also give preference to deep-rooted trees such as oaks over shallow-rooted species such as maples and pines. The roots of the latter will compete for water and nutrients with the roots of plants you put near them.

Whenever possible, don't just cut unwanted deciduous trees down. Many deciduous trees send up shoots after they're cut, so you'll have to keep trimming them until they finally die. If a tree is small, try pulling it out of the ground. If you can't pull it out by yourself, get some help or use a come-along or, if possible, a tractor or other power equipment. If you can pull the tree out roots and all, you'll never have to deal with it again.

If you can't pull a tree out of the ground, you can, of course, cut it down and dig out the roots with a pick and shovel. Grubbing roots, however, is a long, tedious job. It's usually easier to cut the tree off at ground level and snip off shoots as they appear. The sooner you remove new leaves, incidentally, the sooner you deprive the tree of its food supply, and the sooner it dies. On the other hand, the longer you wait, the longer the tree lives and the longer you'll have to deal with it.

You can also try killing the tree with an herbicide such as Round-Up. I rarely use chemical plant killers because I'm afraid of damage they might do to nearby plants that I don't want to harm, and I have an antiherbicide bias: I doubt they're as safe as the people who make and sell them say they are (though I don't question their sincerity). I worry that, twenty or thirty years from now, we'll find out that we were unwittingly doing something horrible to our gardens— or, worse, to ourselves—when we used them. As long as I can kill unwanted plants without chemicals, I will.

Cutting down unwanted trees, incidentally, is usually not very difficult work, because most of the trees you'll be cutting will be small. Most, if not all, can be taken down with a bow saw, so you won't need to buy or rent a power saw. Some towns have ordinances restricting tree removal. Before you start cutting, check to see if any apply to you.

SHRUBS AND FLOWERS Besides trees, you must also decide which shrubs and flowers to leave or remove.

If you live in the Northeast, your woodland may have mountain laurel. If you live in the South or the Pacific Northwest, it may contain rhododendrons. If these or other evergreen shrubs are already growing in your woods, you're lucky: you already have some of the essential plants of the woodland garden that you would otherwise have to buy.

Most woodlands, unfortunately, have few shrubs—evergreen or deciduous—mainly because they tend to be too dark. Besides trees, their only plants are mainly deciduous wildflowers, ground covers, and other low plants growing on or close to the forest floor.

Obviously, some of these plants, such as poison ivy (*Rhus radicans*), poison oak (*Rhus diversiloba*), and nettles (*Urtica*), are pests that must be pulled up. But unlike most small hardwood trees, most smaller plants are not intrinsically objectionable in the woodland garden. Their desirability is based on six tests:

- Is the plant evergreen or deciduous? Deciduous plants are part-time plants. In cold climates, the ground in which they grow is bare (or snow coverd) much of the year. Unfortunately, naturally growing evergreen wildflowers and ground covers—like naturally growing evergreen shrubs—are rare. If you already have pachysandra, vinca, ivy (*Hedera* spp.), wild ginger (*Asarum canadense*), or other evergreen ground covers growing on your property, you're fortunate. You already have plants that—like evergreen shrubs—you would otherwise have to buy. So if it's evergreen, and growing thickly and well, it stays. If it's deciduous, it must pass four more tests.

- Is the plant in the way? Canadian mayflowers, also known as false lily-of-the-valley, are like dozens of other ephemeral spring flowers. They take advantage of the sunlight that shines on the forest floor in the early spring before the tree canopy leafs out. For a month or so they're beautiful. But when the forest darkens after the leaves fill in, they die back, leaving the ground bare until next year. If your woodland garden were filled only with flowers like these, it would be a dull place much of the year. That's why many Canadian mayflowers and spring bloomers like them should be replaced with evergreens. If more than half the floor of your woods is covered with deciduous plants, at least some of them should be replaced with evergreen ground covers.

- Is the plant inherently attractive? When the plant is out of bloom—which it will be most of the time—how does it look? Does it have really attractive leaves? Or, like many non-evergreen plants, is its foliage unremarkable? Is it thick and full or scruffy? On the whole, does it make the garden more or less beautiful?

- Is the plant well located? If the plant is part of a cluster, or drift, of the same plant you may want to leave it because most plants look better in drifts. But if it's a loner, it may appear weak and unimpressive, and the garden may look better without it. If it looks out of place in a drift of another species it definitely has to go.

- Is the plant getting enough sun? Some woodland plants are sparse and leggy because they need more light. Unfortunately for them, most woodlands get darker each year because their leaf canopies get thicker. A forest's natural history is on the side of shade-loving plants. Sun-loving plants will find their time slowly running out. When a plant is no longer suited to its site, pull it up.

- If you're in doubt about a flower, leave it—at least temporarily. You can always remove it later if you decide you really don't like it, but it's hard to put it back after it's been pulled up—especially in the woods. Remember that plants in the wrong place don't always have to be destroyed. Some can be transplanted. If the plant is healthy, if you're able to dig up all or most of its roots, and if you can find a suitable place to move it, you might try transplanting. If you do, make sure the new location is properly prepared.

PRUNING

While some trees in the garden must be removed entirely, others need only to be pruned.

When you prune, you remove branches for several reasons:

- They block a desirable view;
- They may strike someone walking by;
- They are diseased, insect-infested, or otherwise harmful to the tree, including branches rubbing against each other;
- They are dead, badly shaped, or make the tree unattractive.

Dead branches high up in a tall tree are sometimes better left alone. The branches may not be noticeable, it's time-consuming and sometimes dangerous work to remove them, and it's expensive work if you hire a tree surgeon to do it. If you do the work yourself, you have to carry around and carefully position a tall ladder (many times), you have to climb up and down the ladder (many times), you have to cut off the branches (while not falling off the ladder), and you may have to camouflage the light-colored cuts with tree paint. It's much easier just to pick up the branches, on your strolls through the garden, after they fall.

What's more, some trees may actually look better with a few dead branches left on. Many evergreen trees, for example, have long, straight, mastlike trunks that can look homely if they're bare all the way up to the crown. I left dead branches on some of the large white pines in Evergreen, because the branches were picturesque and I thought the tree would look better with them on than with them off. The dead branches also provided some screening, and, not incidentally, leaving them on the tree was much less work than taking them off.

In addition to dead wood, remove branches that spoil a tree's otherwise graceful shape. A deciduous tree is graceful because it tapers: it changes its thickness only gradually from its widest point—the part of the trunk nearest the ground—to its narrowest points—tiny twigs far from the trunk. Watersprouts and suckers are minute branches that must be pruned from a tree because, instead of growing where other lit-

tle branches grow—at the ends of branches only slightly larger than themselves—they spring from parts of the tree many times larger than they are. Suckers grow from or near the base of the tree; watersprouts usually spring from major limbs (see figure 1).

You should also prune branches that are out of place in other ways: those that are much longer than surrounding limbs, that grow in markedly different directions from those around them or that, in any way, are out of harmony with the rest of the tree.

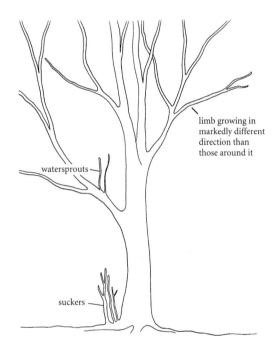

limb growing in markedly different direction than those around it

watersprouts

suckers

FIGURE 1: *To make a deciduous tree more graceful, prune suckers, waterspouts, and limbs that grow in a markedly different direction from those around them.*

You prune trees for the same reason that you cut them down: to let more sunlight into the garden. In fact, pruning a big tree for this purpose may be an easier and faster alternative than cutting down and removing the whole thing.

Trees can also be pruned to make them fuller. In a search for more light, trees growing in the shade of the woodland canopy tend to produce long, thin branches with relatively few leaves scattered along the stems. Unfortunately, a tree with too many long, thin branches and sparse leaf cover is often unattractive. By cutting parts of the branches off, you can produce new, more concentrated leaf and stem growth closer to the tree. Don't remove more than a third of a tree's total leaf or needle mass at one time, however, or the tree may die.

When you prune, make sure your tools are sharp so you can make clean cuts. (Ragged cuts expose the tree to rot and disease.) Hold the branch you're cutting to make sure it doesn't fall and tear bark off the tree. If the limb is too heavy to hold in place, remove it with three cuts:

1. A partial cut on the bottom of the branch, a few inches away from the trunk to prevent the branch from tearing off bark from the tree when it falls.
2. A cut on the top of the branch, a bit farther away from the trunk than the first cut, to remove most of the limb.
3. A cut close to the trunk, but outside the collar (the swelling at the base of the limb), to remove the rest of the branch. (The first cut can't remove the limb because, if the branch is heavy enough, its weight will bind the saw.) Make the third cut perpendicular to the edge of the branch, not at an angle, so the cut will be as small as possible (see figure 2).

If the light color of a cut is unsightly or if the cut is more than an inch across, cover it with antiseptic tree paint. The paint makes the cut less obvious, protects the tree from insects and disease, and seals the wound so the tree won't leak sap.

DEBRIS REMOVAL

When you clean up, weed, and prune your woods, you've got to get rid of the debris. There are several alternatives:

- Haul it (or have it hauled) to a landfill or other dump site;
- Grind green wood into chips for mulch;
- Cut larger pieces for firewood (if they haven't started to rot);
- Use it to fill unwanted hollows and holes;

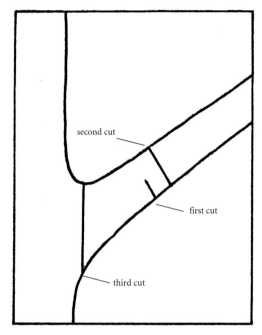

second cut

first cut

third cut

FIGURE 2: *When pruning a heavy limb, begin by making a partial cut on the bottom of the branch, then make a cut on the top, and finally make a cut close to the tree.*

can dispose of it in the woods by hiding it, burning it, or using it for fill.

MAKING FIREWOOD If you have a wood stove or fireplace and if, like me, you hate to throw anything away, you may want to burn anything that's relatively accessible and isn't rotten. Remember that pines and other pitch-heavy evergreens can leave a lot of creosote in a chimney (especially if the fire isn't burning very hot) and that creosote causes chimney fires. Some people burn it anyway; they insist that, if the fire is hot enough and if the chimney is cleaned often enough, there's no problem. Others (including me) think that's a reckless idea and use softwood only for kindling, if at all If you want to play it safe, burn only hardwood indoors. And avoid burning hardwoods like elm that produce a foul-smelling fire.

⚘ Bury it under ramps or berms;
⚘ Hide it on the site;
⚘ Burn dry wood in a brushfire.

The method or methods you use to get rid of your debris will partly depend on where it is. If, for example, it's near your house or a road, it's relatively easy to haul it away or gather it up for firewood or chips.

If, on the other hand, it's several hundred feet or more from your house or a road, you may have neither the time nor the energy to drag it out of the woods. In that case you

MAKING CHIPS Freshly cut trees can be ground up into wood chips for mulch. (Unfortunately, most dead wood can't be ground up because it's so dry that it quickly dulls the blades of a chipping machine.) Depending on where you live, wood chips cost roughly eight to twelve dollars a cubic yard if you pick them up yourself and about sixteen to twenty dollars a yard if they're delivered to your house—and that's only when you buy at least six yards. But if you rent a large (fifteen-or-more-horsepower) chipper (for about forty dollars a day) you can chip your own mulch. If you have a lot of trees to grind up, renting a chipper is cheaper than buying chips.

To maximize your savings, get all your tree weeding and pruning done and all the debris carried out of the woods before you rent the chipper. Start early enough so you can chip all your trees in one day.

You can, of course, buy your own chipper. But even the smallest, cheapest models cost more than $1,000 and they can chip only small branches (usually only two inches thick or less). They also take longer than bigger machines to do it. That's why it's usually wiser to rent a chipper than buy one.

You might also be tempted to hire a tree surgeon to chip your brush for you, but that's usually not a good idea either. It's expensive to haul a chipper around and it takes time to chip many small stems. Usually, the chips you get this way will cost more than the same quantity delivered to your home.

BURYING DEBRIS If you have holes or hollows that would look better filled in, you can dispose of brush in them. Remember, however, that you have to hide the debris by throwing dirt over it, and hauling dirt in a wheelbarrow over a woodland path is harder than dragging brush. You may want to bury your debris only when the hole you have to fill is deep: so deep that you can bury a large amount of debris under the dirt.

If you plan to build a berm—and rare is the garden that doesn't need at least one—you're in luck. Berms and ramps are excellent places to get rid of brush. Just drag it to where the ramp or berm is going to be built and drop it. The fill will cover it nicely. (Berm and ramp construction are discussed in Step Three.)

HIDING DEBRIS Another way to dispose of brush is simply to hide it: find a place where no one (including your neighbors) will see it—almost certainly outside the gardened area of the woods—and pile it there. Eventually the brush will decompose and rot away. In fact, if you'd like to build a compost pile, this may be the place to do it. Even if you don't actively compost the wood, it will eventually turn into humus-rich soil all by itself.

The outside slope of a berm—the slope farthest away from the garden and closest to the boundary of the property—is one handy hiding place for brush. Not only will the brush not be seen from inside the garden, it will also reduce the angle of the outside slope of the berm, giving more protection to the roots of shrubs planted there. As the brush decays, its humus will enrich the soil on the berm.

BURNING DEBRIS The only other way to dispose of dead wood in the woods is to burn it in a brushfire. Before you strike a match, however, check with your local fire department. They'll tell you what you must do to obey local ordinances. They may also give you some tips on how to burn your brush safely. In case they don't, here are a few suggestions:

- Make sure the only thing you burn is brush. Build your fires in relatively open areas, where the flames won't spread to tree trunks or overhead branches. Rake up fallen leaves, needles, twigs, and other forest duff around the fire site so they won't ignite. If the ground is dry, run a hose to the site and soak the soil with water. Keep a hose or other water handy while you're burning.

- Keep your fires small. Small fires are easier to control than large ones. Also, small fires are especially welcome when burning large pieces of wood—trunks of big trees, for example—that are too big to carry out of the woods easily. Simply roll or push big chunks of wood where you can safely build a small fire around them, add enough brush for kindling, and ignite.

- Burn when the wind is calm, usually early evening.
- Never leave a fire unattended.
- If the brush isn't dry enough, douse it with some kind of fuel, such as charcoal lighter, kerosene, gasoline, or used motor oil. Make sure you stand clear when you ignite it.

A brush fire is the most time-consuming way to get rid of wood. Most other methods require only moving the debris to a certain place and simply leaving it. Burning requires additional (and occasionally dangerous and often tedious) steps: getting an often reluctant fire to start, watching it for several hours before it finally burns out, then disposing of the inevitable pieces that refuse to burn up. These are three good reasons why you should burn your dead wood only as a last resort.

Although gardening by subtraction isn't expensive, it's hard work. In small doses this work is fun, even invigorating. But dragging armload after armload of brush through the woods may sometimes make you feel like Sisyphus—a good reason for doing only a little of the work at a time, gardening only a part of your woods at once, hiring someone to do some or all of the work, or moving some of the brush with a truck or tractor. Hiring help is an attractive idea because removing brush is unskilled labor and you can usually hire people for reasonable wages. Using power equipment can make the work easier, too, if at least some of the site is accessible to it.

Cleaning up, weeding, and pruning Evergreen was a relatively easy job for several reasons:

- Many of the rocks and trees on the site didn't have to be removed. On the contrary, they were prized possessions.
- Because the property is a mature, shady woods, undesirable understory plants such as shrubs and small deciduous trees were few and often small.
- I allowed many small but well-shaped deciduous trees to remain because I valued their warm yellow fall foliage and their ability to help screen neighboring houses when they were leafed out.
- All the brush was handily disposed of in berms, many of which were not far from where the brush was cut.

What exactly had to be removed?

For one thing, rocks. For every handsome boulder on the site, there were at least two small stones (smaller than basketballs) that were simply litter.

Also, small hardwood trees. Growing beneath the big pines were many witch hazels—small gangly trees that added little to the beauty of the landscape. Their many spindly stems grew diagonally, not vertically, spoiling the striking verticality created by the pines' massive, straight trunks.

I also removed small white pines and minute small-leafed deciduous trees, such as cherry and ash. Many were skinny and obviously starved for light under the canopy of the pines. Like the witch hazels, they contributed only clutter to the site.

Growing in and along the brook were many honeysuckle bushes (*Lonicera*)—homely woody deciduous shrubs, also starved for light, that hid the brook and made it nearly inaccessible. Other unwelcome plants were a few wild raspberries and some thick patches of poison ivy farther upstream.

There were also several dozen dead trees—some standing, many fallen—throughout the property and lots of branches on the ground. The largest collection of dead wood was created by a previous

Opposite: Pachysandra and handsome moss-covered rocks line the paths on the West Bank of the brook at Evergreen (notice the mountain laurel on the left). Barberries grow along the path on the East Bank (rear).

owner of the house to the east. He had cut several large white pines on his property and had thrown what seemed like two truckloads of logs and branches over the cliffs. The brush covered up the lower part of the cliffs and, like the honeysuckles, hid much of the brook.

Finally, there was a children's playhouse close to the north side of the house. The building was attractive enough—a tiny, brown-stained wooden cabin with a window, window box, and Dutch door— but it was too much of a focal point. It sucked attention away from the trees and shrubs and made the garden look too, for lack of a better word, "developed." My carpenter agreed to remove the house for free. (He reassembled it in his own yard as a playhouse for his young son and daughter.)

Many of the standing dead trees were pines. Pines have shallow roots, enabling me to get rid of many simply by pushing them over, roots and all (sometimes after a little rocking). Because most of the standing dead deciduous trees were small (actually, they were dead because they were small—too small to get enough light), they could be yanked out of the ground roots and all, just like the pines. Only a few dead trees had to be cut down with a bow saw. (None were large enough to require a chain saw.)

Other plants had to be weeded out. All the honeysuckles, all the cherries, ashes, and other tiny, small-leafed deciduous trees, and all but a few of the witch hazels and small pines were removed.

The honeysuckles all had large crowns but small, weak roots, so they came up effortlessly and when they did—*voila!*— there was the brook underneath, burbling beautifully over its rocky bed.

The long vines of poison ivy came up easily, too. The trick is to pull up every one you see and keep pulling them up every time they reappear. Eventually they'll disappear.

If you're allergic to poison ivy—and most people are—be sure not to touch it. Wear gloves, long sleeves, long pants—cover any part of your body that might touch it— and try not to rub your face or any other exposed part of your body while you're working. Despite all these precautions, however, the poison ivy may still touch bare skin. I recommend a soapy shower—with emphasis on hands, arms, face, and other suspected contact points—immediately after pulling up poison ivy (and within an hour of first handling it). It takes a while for the oil in the plant to do its dirty work. If you can remove it in time, you're usually safe. Use green soap tincture, a liquid detergent sold in most drug stores; it's more powerful than ordinary facial soap. Be sure to wash everything—clothes, tools, etc.— that may have touched the poison ivy; these things can pass the toxins along, too.

A large drift of hay-scented ferns growing under Evergreen's large white pines was a gift of nature I chose to keep. 'Roseum Elegans' rhododendrons bloom in the foreground, and the White and Gold rooms are in the distance.

Many of the other shrubs and many of the smallest trees were also uprooted. The larger trees, of course, had to be cut down. Because deciduous trees sprout after they're cut, I had to snip off the sprouts several times a year for two or three years before the trees died completely.

I also had to deal with an impressive drift of hay-scented ferns. A twenty-foot-square drift was the largest fern bed on the property. Another generous gift of nature, unfortunately, its unnaturally square shape was appropriate for a formal garden but not for this one.

This witch hazel provides warm fall color at Evergreen. Its graceful shape is a result of careful pruning—a good example of gardening by subtraction.

For a while, I wasn't sure what to do about the large patch of ferns. I didn't want to try transplanting them because it's almost impossible to dig them out of rooty woodland soil without doing them great harm. But I also didn't want to leave them in place. Then the idea struck. It was another version of gardening by subtraction. From the northwest corner of the patch to the southeast corner, I cut a gently curving S-shaped path. Now, instead of a big, dull, formal square bed of ferns, I have two graceful, irregularly curving clusters, one each side of the path. What's more, I have a delightful fifteen-foot walkway bordered on both sides by luscious, three-foot-tall ferns.

Besides cleaning up and weeding, I also pruned several trees on the site. A gigantic white pine and a maple tree on the north side of the house were pruned heavily to allow more sunlight to shine on two fishponds nearby. The extra light allowed waterlilies in the pond to bloom.

I also pruned the lower branches off the deciduous trees on the banks of the brook to open up views of the cliffs edging the eastern side of the garden, but I carefully left the top branches alone to hide the houses on top of the cliffs. Some of these specimens are considered "weed" or "junk" trees—alder, sumac, locust, etc. But I don't care. I treasure every one of them and hope they send out bigger and bigger masses of leaves every year. I need them all—and actually a few more—to hide the houses behind them.

I also pruned a couple of witch hazels on my neighbor's property (with his permission) so I could have a view of some huge, handsome rocks on his land. (I was careful not to cut other branches that hid another neighbor's house farther south.)

A witch hazel near the northwest corner of the garden was pruned to give it a simple, gracefully arching shape. Another witch hazel was shaped to provide variety and interest to the center of a space near the Cave. A third one, beside the large pool in the brook, was pruned to frame an upstream view of the stream. All three trees also help screen houses next door.

When I was done cleaning up, weeding, and pruning, the garden already looked so much better than it did when I first saw it. And I hadn't added a single plant! As a result of just gardening by subtraction, I had created a clean, open, parklike woodland dominated by massive white pines and huge handsome granite rocks. If I had stopped right there, I would already have had an elegant idealized woodland. But the next three steps made Evergreen even better.

GRADING—MAKING PATHS, RAMPS, AND BERMS

Not surprisingly, much of garden-making involves plants. Grading is different. It's about dirt, or, more precisely, it's about using fill and loam to make paths, ramps, and berms.

Ramps take you up and down steep grades. Together with paths, they make it easy to walk around the garden and they lead you to its best views. Berms make the garden more private by screening it from houses and other development around it.

PATHS

When you walk through a woodland garden, you'll almost always be walking on a path. That's why everything you see in the garden you'll either see from a path or you won't see it at all. So a path isn't just a walkway that takes you to different parts of the garden. It's also a linear observation platform. It must be laid out so it shows you the garden at its best: it must offer the best views possible, as often as possible.

What's more, a garden path must not only be scenic. It must also be smooth and gentle. The beauty of a garden can be enjoyed most when it can be savored easily and when you can give your full attention to it—when you don't have to worry about tripping over rocks or roots, stepping in mud or water, or getting branches in your eye—and when you don't have to trudge up or lurch down a steep path. The ideal garden path must be as smooth and level as possible: so smooth and so gentle that you barely notice it, so smooth that you can take it for granted, like a sidewalk. There should be nothing beneath your feet to spoil the pleasures of the garden or to detract your attention from them.

Happily, the foot traffic on most residential garden paths is light enough so they don't need paving. That's good, because paving has two liabilities: it's costly and it makes the garden look unnatural. Even relatively informal pavings such as stones or wood chips are obviously manmade additions that compromise a garden's natural appearance.

Fortunately, the dirt floor of most woods makes a fine path all by itself. It's softer and cooler than concrete, asphalt, or crushed stone, and it can be made as smooth and as dry as any other surface.

Putting the path in the right place is essential. In fact, paths are not as much made as they are chosen. The easiest, cheapest, and most natural way to have a smooth, dry, and level path is to choose one that's smooth, dry, and relatively level to begin with.

Unfortunately, nature rarely provides the perfect path, so you'll almost always have to do at least a little grooming. Grooming means removing or covering up anything anyone might fall into, trip over, bump into, or get stuck to their shoes.

Holes should be filled in. Rough spots should be smoothed over, usually by adding loam (or whatever fill most closely matches the color of the path) and raking it smooth. Stones and other debris should be picked up. Roots and rocks too big to be removed should be covered with dirt. Muddy spots should be filled in with a layer of sand and the sand covered with dirt that matches the rest of the path. If the sand is higher than the level of the surrounding water, the top of the path should be dry.

You should also trim any branches that anyone might bump into, including those less than three feet from the path and lower than seven feet from the ground.

Some parts of a woodland may be too rocky to walk through. In that case, you won't be able to simply choose a path—you'll have to build one. Sometimes you can create a smooth walkway by removing the rocks. More often, it's easier just to add fill. Simply add enough fill to cover the rocks so that a footway is wide enough to walk on comfortably; a two-foot width is sufficient. Cover the fill with dirt that matches the soil around it.

If your path must go up or down a slope, try to route it along a grade so gentle that, when you walk on it, you'll have no sense of going up or down. Any sensation that you are climbing (up or down), any sense in your legs that you are doing anything but simply walking, is an intrusion upon your experience of the garden, and it will detract from the quality of that experience.

Unless a path must go to the top of a hill (to a viewpoint, for example) route the path around the hill. In fact, let your path meander around every little hump. Remember, the idea isn't to get there quickly. It's to get there easily—and in the most scenic way.

If you must ascend a hill, try not to take the path directly up the slope. Instead, take it diagonally across the hill, like a hiking trail that traverses the slope of a mountain. If the slope is long, and you can't ascend it in one traverse, switch the path back and forth in a series of traverses, like hairpin turns on a mountain road.

If the slope is very steep, cut a shelf in the hillside so the width of the path will be level. If the ground is relatively root-free, you can level the path by a simple process known as "cutting and filling." Simply dig, or "cut," into the hillside on the up-slope side of the path, then use the cut soil to raise, or "fill," the down-slope side of the path (see figure 3). If the ground is rooty and can't be readily dug, it may be easier to bring in new soil to fill the down-slope side of the path.

In any case, always remember to resist the all-too-common tendency to take the shortest distance between two points. Always ask yourself as you lay out a path: is this the most level possible grade? Or is there a gentler alternative to the right or the left? While you're building your paths, you may be working too hard to notice their grades. But you'll surely notice them when you're strolling through the garden.

Paths that go around rather than over hills are not only easier on the body, they also tend to produce more attractive gardens. The lower a path is, the higher are the trees and shrubs around it and, therefore,

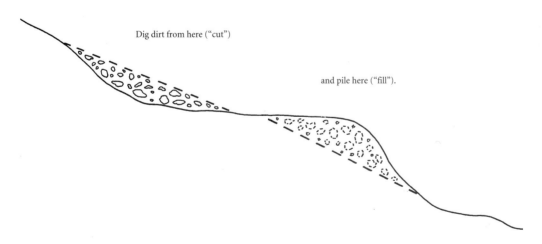

Dig dirt from here ("cut")

and pile here ("fill").

FIGURE 3: *Level a path on a hillside by "cutting-and-filling." "Cut" fill from the up-slope side of a path and use it to "fill" the down-slope side.*

the larger and lusher the garden looks and feels when you walk through it.

Because they're longer than straight paths, meandering paths take more time to walk, therefore extending the experience of the garden and making the garden seem larger and richer.

Winding paths also make a garden more interesting than straight paths through "progressive realization." Unlike a straight path, a path that curves through the garden lets you see only a little of it at a time. It shows you a bit of the garden after one curve, a little more after the next, and so on. In other words you "realize" the views not all at once but gradually or "progressively." A "progressively realized" view is always changing, so it's always fresh and never boring.

A meandering path is always fresh, too. No part of it ever seems too long—because no part ever is. If you've ever walked on the long, wide, flat, arrow-straight allées of eighteenth-century formal gardens you know how tedious, even onerous, those supposedly pleasant walks can be. (Those at the La Granja palace near Madrid are especially annoying, partly because they also go

Opposite: White and yellow azaleas flank a path into an evergreen forest at the Bloedel Reserve. Epimedium covers the ground beneath the azaleas.

unrelentingly uphill. Their merit is that they teach us exactly what a good garden path is not!)

Unfortunately, hills are not the only things a path must negotiate. Large rocks and trees; brooks, ponds, and other bodies of water; and natural features that can't or shouldn't be removed may make a smooth, gently graded path impossible.

A path may have to take the steeper way down a hill because the more level route is blocked by a boulder or a rare, lovely stand of mountain laurel. Sometimes the smoothest path will also be the steepest, or the more level path will also be narrow or rocky. In cases like these, choose the greater good. If you can't have a perfect path, at least you can have the best path possible.

Most of the paths in Evergreen needed little work. Much of the garden has a smooth surface (often covered with pine needles), and I was able to lay out most of the paths across level, nearly level, or very gentle grades. Some stones had to be removed and branches trimmed out of the way, but virtually no fill was needed.

Several paths, however, required special work.

I wanted to be able to walk easily alongside the brook so I could have continuing views of the water. I also wanted to be as close as possible to the stream so its impact would be as powerful as possible and where what naturalist John Muir called the "singing" of its cascades would be as loud as it could be.

Unfortunately, much of the stream bank was rough and rocky. You could pick your way over it, of course, but the experience was more like rock climbing than strolling effortlessly through a garden.

The solution was simple: build a smooth dirt path over the rocks on the bank where the stream was the most accessible.

First, I moved a few barberry bushes out of the way by transplanting them farther away from the brook. Then my helpers and I brought a few dozen wheelbarrow loads of fill down to the stream and dumped them along the brook—within a couple of feet of the water, but far enough away and high enough above the brook so the fill wouldn't be washed away. I raked the fill smooth, making sure it had a slight slope to shed rainwater into the stream. Next, I tamped the fill down and placed a few stones where they were needed to make sure the brook wouldn't reach the new path. Finally, I added a thin layer of loam to make the path look like it had been there all along.

Now you can stroll effortlessly along the entire length of the brook, just inches from the stream, and enjoy water-filled vistas both upstream and down.

I also had to grade the path across the wide, steep slope on the West Bank of the brook. The path itself isn't steep—in fact it climbs very slowly. The surface of the path, however, climbed the steep grade of the hill—so steep that it twisted your feet when you walked on it.

Cutting and filling was out of the question because it would have disturbed too many roots. That would have been hard on me and hard on the roots. Instead of cutting and filling, I opted for just filling. My helpers dumped fill along the downhill edge of the path, and I leveled it out with a rake. The fill makes the downhill side of the path higher, so the entire surface of the path is now more level. The footing is now flat enough to walk on comfortably but still sloping enough to shed rainwater easily and keep the path dry. Like all fill-made paths, this one was covered, for cosmetic reasons, with a layer of loam.

Two short sections of path did not merely have to cross steep grades, they had to ascend them. There was no room for the paths to climb the slopes diagonally, in a single traverse—the hills were too narrow— so the paths had to go almost directly uphill. I made the trails ascend the hillsides in a series of easy switchbacks, adding fill and loam to make the footing more level. I further defined the paths (and made sure people stayed on them) by planting shrubs and ground cover on both sides.

RAMPS, OR MAKING YOUR OWN GRADE

If you need a route down a cliff or bluff that's too rough or steep for any path, even one with switchbacks, you'll have to replace the precipitous original grade with a more gentle artificial one. You'll have to build an earth ramp.

A ramp is a simple structure. It's nothing more than dirt dumped on the bottom of a steep slope to make the grade gentler (see figure 4).

A ramp should be built only as a last resort because, even though it's simple, it still costs much more (in time and materials) to build than a path.

On the other hand, an earth ramp has many advantages over anything else:

- ☙ It's faster, cheaper, and easier to build than stairs, steps, or a concrete ramp.
- ☙ Because it's dirt, it costs virtually nothing to maintain—unlike wood or masonry.
- ☙ It looks natural—unlike steps, stairs, or wood or concrete structures.

☙ Like any good path, a ramp takes much less concentration to negotiate than stairs or steps so it interferes less with the enjoyment of the garden.

To build an earth ramp, dump fill on the bottom of the slope. Keep adding fill until the grade of the ramp is gentle enough to ascend and descend comfortably. Make the ramp wide enough for one person to walk on easily—at least two feet.

To make the ramp look natural, make it irregular—slightly curving instead of straight, wider in some places, narrower in others—and vary the grade of the slopes on either side of the path. Cover the whole thing with loam to make it look like the rest of the paths and plant its slopes like any other part of the garden.

If, for some reason, you don't have space for a ramp and you have to build steps

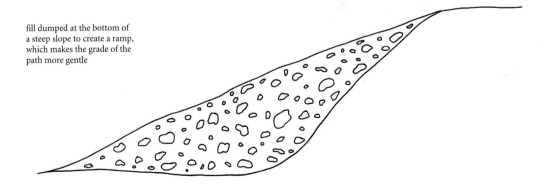

fill dumped at the bottom of a steep slope to create a ramp, which makes the grade of the path more gentle

FIGURE 4: *Make a path up a steep grade gentler by building a ramp, which is nothing more than fill dumped at the bottom of the slope.*

The berm on the left, planted with vinca, pachysandra, rhododendrons, and a mugo pine, helps screen Evergreen from the street. Japanese andromeda and mountain andromeda are seen on the right.

instead, make the steps harmonize with the garden as much as possible. The best way to do this is by building them out of stones found on the site, which are usually similar to each other in color and texture. If there aren't enough usable stones on the property, substitute others that resemble them as closely as possible.

Logs are a slightly less harmonious material because, while stones are usually found on the floor of the garden, logs usually are not. Logs also have three other disadvantages: They rot, they're slippery when they're wet, and their sawn ends make them look unnatural. If you do use them, make sure the sawn ends are covered with dirt so they can't be seen.

In any event, don't build steps out of unnatural-looking materials such as bricks, lumber, or concrete blocks. Their flat planes, square corners, and obviously man-made appearance is appropriate for artificial creations such as houses but not for natural-looking woodland gardens. Garden centers may tell you that railroad ties are appropriate "landscaping timbers" but sawn wood is no better for woodland gardens than bricks or concrete blocks. Concrete should be used only to bond stones and as much of it as possible should be hidden. Remember, a woodland garden is for getting away from the manmade world, not for duplicating it.

Although Evergreen is a hilly garden—its highest point is at least fifty feet higher than its lowest point—there are no flights of steps in it. In fact, the only outdoor stairs on the entire property are concrete-and-flagstone steps leading to the front and side entrances of the house. Instead of steps, there are two ramps in the garden, each built on a slope that was too steep and narrow for even switchbacking paths.

One ramp was built where a path now descends into the woods from the driveway. Fill was pushed down the bluff with a bulldozer, then raked farther downhill to make a long, wide, gentle slope that curves between several trees.

The other ramp was built where a path descends into the woods from the lawn in front of my house. The spot was too far from the driveway for a bulldozer to reach, so I carried about twenty cubic yards of fill to the site in a wheelbarrow. When the ramp was high enough, I smoothed it out with a rake, then added a layer of topsoil. Now I have a wide, flat slope planted with rhododendrons, pachysandra, and vinca. The path curves between the evergreen plantings on the ramp and the trunk of a massive white pine at the edge of the lawn.

The original owners of the property had built a steep flight of stone-and-concrete steps where the ramp is now. The narrow steps were tricky to negotiate even when they were new. Forty years later, when I bought the property, they were crumbling. Unlike the hapless steps, my ramps look

natural, are easy to ascend and descend, will last indefinitely, and cost only about $200 worth of dirt to build.

BERMS, OR MAKING YOUR OWN RIDGES

If you can see some of your neighbors' homes from your garden, your garden needs at least one berm. A berm is a linear mound of earth, shaped like a small ridge. Built along the edge of a garden, it blocks views of houses, cars, streets, and telephone poles and reduces the noise of traffic, people, dogs, radios, etc. By insulating your garden against these and other scourges of residential development, a berm helps maintain the garden's integrity and natural character. A berm allows a garden's views of rocks, water, trees, shrubs and other natural things to be unadulterated by views of manmade things.

Hedges, walls, and fences can also screen the garden from intrusions, but a berm is by far the best insulator of all, for these reasons:

- Berms are solid, blocking views completely. Most hedges don't because they have spaces between their branches and leaves. Also, deciduous hedges lose most of their screening power in the fall, when their leaves fall off.
- Berms are more dense than hedges and fences and thicker than fences,

walls, and virtually any hedge, so they usually block sound better than any other barrier.

⚛ Unlike hedges, fences, and walls, berms can be planted with trees and shrubs to provide more and higher screening.

⚛ Berms can be made any height and still be attractive. (After all, they look just like a ridge or small hill.) On the other hand, fences and walls are usually eyesores if they're more than eight feet tall, and an eight-foot barrier usually can't hide a building if the structure is more than one story high.

⚛ Berms are cheaper to install than walls or fences of equal height.

⚛ Hedges need pruning; fences need painting, staining, and regular rebuilding; and masonry walls need repointing. Berms need no maintenance at all. After all, how could they wear out? They're dirt.

⚛ Berms are not just practical, they're interesting landforms. Their gentle hilly shapes provide welcome relief from the often boring flatness of the typical yard. Unlike fences, walls, or formal hedges, a well-designed, well-planted berm looks natural, like a little ridge. It looks great in a woodland garden. Fences and walls never look natural—because they're not.

⚛ The slopes of berms are almost ideal platforms to display plants. On level surfaces plants are often hidden by other plants in front of them. On berms plants cover much less, and sometimes nothing at all, of the plants behind them. Because berms raise plants off the floor and up the walls of the outdoor room, they distribute them more widely throughout the three dimensions of the garden, making the garden seem fuller and more lush.

⚛ Some people think walls and fences are unfriendly and unneighborly, especially if they're unattractive. Berms are different. They create privacy—just like walls and fences—but they don't look like privacy barriers. Walls and solid fences are tall, flat, vertical, sometimes ugly, and obviously manmade obstructions that—not surprisingly—look like privacy barriers. Berms, on the other hand, look like what they are: rich, well-textured gardens composed of graceful landforms thickly planted with handsome trees and shrubs. Many look so natural that they seem as if they were always there.

Unlike fences and walls, berms are very neighborly. What is

Fuchsia azaleas create an exciting contrast along the pine needle-carpeted Azalea Trails of Callaway Gardens.

unneighborly about a handsome arrangement of trees and shrubs? In fact, isn't a front yard with lots of trees and shrubs usually more interesting, more beautiful, and for those reasons, more neighborly than a front yard composed of little more than a large, wide, plain, flat lawn?

In many communities walls and fences are illegal if they're over a certain height or too close to the street or property boundary. Berms are usually unregulated. You can build them high enough to provide all the screening you need.

How a berm is built depends on where it's built. If the site is near a road or otherwise accessible to heavy equipment, trucks can haul in the earth, and a bulldozer or similar earth-moving machine can grade it into a ridgelike shape.

If the site is surrounded by trees or otherwise inaccessible to heavy machinery, construction is more difficult. In that case you have a choice: You can carry the dirt to the site in a wheelbarrow and grade the berm with a shovel and rake, or you can make the site accessible to machinery by building an access road. The wider the road, the bigger the machinery that can reach the site. (A six-foot-wide road is big enough for a Bobcat, a bulldozer needs nine feet, and a dump truck at least ten.)

Building a road is usually pricey and, ironically, might destroy much of the garden you are creating—including valuable trees. Building the berm by hand, however, is slow, hard work. But it's also unskilled work and you can almost certainly hire people at modest wages to help you do it.

Luckily, berms are usually most needed not deep in the woods, where the sights and sounds of civilization are less likely to intrude, but along a street or road, where those sights and sounds are close by. This makes many berms easy to build: dump trucks can simply drive up and drop their loads along the edge of the property, and a bulldozer can usually get close enough to shape the earth. Only the final grooming has to be done by hand.

Most woodland gardens need only modest-size berms. Usually six to twelve feet of dirt, plus a top planting of trees or shrubs will provide enough screening.

Even if you can't make your berm high enough to exclude every unwelcome sight and sound, it will hardly be a failure. On the contrary, it will be a success if it screens any intrusion or even any part of one. If you can't screen every unwelcome vista and noise, you should try to block out as many as possible. If you can't create perfect privacy, you can create as much privacy as possible.

To make a berm look natural, make it irregular and gently graded—at least twice as wide as it is high, and ideally even wider. Don't make a berm look like a wedge: knife-edged at the top, flat on the sides, and straight from end to end (see figure 5). Shape it like a miniature mountain range. Its crest should undulate, sweeping from low passes to high peaks. The grade of its slopes should vary in steepness and they should all include both convex spurs and concave creases. The entire berm should curve irregularly from end to end (see figure 6).

FIGURE 5: *Don't build a berm like this—knife-edged at the top, flat on the sides, and straight from end to end . . .*

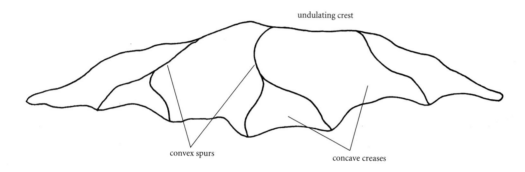

FIGURE 6: *. . . instead, shape it like a miniature mountain range, with an undulating crest, slopes that are steeper than others, and convex spurs and concave creases.*

If a berm has to be built close to a tree, try not to pile too much fill around it. Ideally, you should keep dirt away from a tree all the way to its drip line, which is the widest spread of its foliage. If you cover this area with too much fill, the roots of the tree (which are within the drip line) will not get enough water and air, and the tree will die. If you cover only half of the roots with only a few inches of topsoil, a healthy tree will probably survive. But if you cover all the roots with a foot of topsoil, the tree's chances are dicey. And if you cover all the roots with three or more feet of topsoil, the tree is probably a goner.

You can mitigate this danger by installing a network of perforated pipes above a tree's roots before covering both them and the pipes with dirt. The pipes are designed to bring both air and water to the roots. This procedure—best done by a professional arborist—is an added expense and

it's by no means guaranteed, especially when the roots are covered with several feet of dirt. On the other hand, if you don't install the pipes, the tree may die anyway (if you've put down too much dirt) and your garden will have one less screening element where you most need it. Plus you'll have to remove a dead tree.

The loss of a tree (or several trees), however, may be acceptable. After all, you'd still have the berm. And by the time the tree dies, the trees or shrubs planted on top of the berm will have grown large enough to provide a lot of screening themselves. Plus, you'll still have all the other trees in or around the garden that were unaffected by the berm.

Another alternative is to build a smaller berm that wouldn't threaten any trees. But a smaller berm with more trees left standing would probably provide less screening than a larger berm and fewer trees.

Still another alternative is to make the berm steeper and more narrow, so it won't cover as many roots. A narrow berm won't look as natural as a wider one, but its steep sides can be partly hidden and softened by planting shrubs on them.

Opposite: This path at Evergreen enters the woods through an allée of ferns and 'Emerald Gaiety' euonymus. Notice the rhododendrons under the trees in the distance.

A berm, in other words, may require a tradeoff. You may have to decide whether adding a certain size or shape berm (and its plantings) while subtracting one or more trees will give you more net screening and be more attractive than building a different size or shape berm. That decision, in turn, will depend on the size and location of the things you want to screen and the size, location, and condition of your trees.

In most cases, adding a berm will more than offset any loss of trees, and a higher, more narrow berm, properly planted, will be more valuable than a wider berm providing less screening.

Although my lot is only .8 acres in size and surrounded by other houses, several things help keep those houses out of view, preserving the natural character of the site.

One is the position of my house. Unlike my neighbors' homes, which are all parallel to the street, my house is perpendicular: its long sides face the garden, not the street. The short side that does face the street contains a guest apartment and an extra bedroom, neither of which I use. So from virtually every window I usually look through, I can see only trees and shrubs instead of houses and cars.

Outside, my view is still largely nature, not development, because much of the civilization around my garden is screened by the trees on and around my lot. From May until October, while the deciduous trees are leafed out, the tree screen is so thick that I can hardly see nearby homes to the east (above the brook). Another neighbor's house is partially hidden by the shape of the land—it's higher up the slope to the north—and it's partially camouflaged by its rich brown color.

Unfortunately, the houses to the south and those on the west side of the street were not screened at all when I moved in. And the houses to the north and east became quite visible when the deciduous trees dropped their leaves. In short, my lot was too small to have natural privacy, so I had to create it. I had to build berms on the northern, western, and southern boundaries of my property and in several places in the eastern part of the garden.

The sites of two berms—one near the street on the west side of the lot and one along the driveway near the southwest corner of the property—could be reached by heavy equipment, so a contractor was able to build them with dump trucks and a bulldozer.

My helpers and I began by piling cleanup and weeding debris in long rows along the centers of what would be the bottom of the berms. This not only got rid of my garden waste, it also clearly indicated to the contractor exactly where the berms were to be built.

The piles of debris were covered with about thirty truckloads (or three hundred cubic yards) of fill. Some of the fill was an ordinary mix of sand and clay, which cost seven dollars a cubic yard in 1989, delivered. The rest of the fill was what Scott Rossiter, proprietor of Bedford Sand & Gravel, calls "junk." Junk is what's left after topsoil is screened to produce "screened" loam. As the loam falls through the screen, like flour through a sieve, the "junk"—logs, branches, stumps, some dirt, and whatever else was in the original load—is left on top of the screen. Scott sold the "junk" to me for three dollars a cubic yard, delivered—less than half the price of dirt fill. The woody junk, deep in the ground, decays very slowly, if at all, so the berm settles very little and very gradually, if at all. This settling is acceptable because berms have to support only plants, not buildings, and because any loss of height due to settling is more than offset by growth in the shrubs on top of them. Also, berms made of "junk" are literally less than dirt cheap.

After the fill was dumped, Scott, who is an artist with a bulldozer, shaped it into long, narrow ridges as much as fourteen feet high. Then he covered the ridges with a nine-inch layer of good quality unscreened loam. The unscreened loam had little "junk" in it, so it was suitable for planting shrubs and ground covers, and it's cheaper than screened loam. In 1989, it cost only ten dollars a cubic yard, delivered; screened loam was twelve dollars.

Red azaleas are a brilliant accent on the edge of the Azalea Trails woodlands at Callaway Gardens.

When Scott was done, I smoothed out the loam with a rake, removing any debris as I worked. When finished, the berms totalled about one hundred feet long, were between four and fourteen feet high, and averaged about twelve feet high.

All other berms on the property were too deep in the woods to be reached by trucks or bulldozers. They had to be built by hand.

After cleanup and weeding debris was piled where the berms were to be built, they were covered with fill.

Dump trucks dumped the dirt in my driveway. Then my helpers shoveled it into wheelbarrows, pushed it through the woods, and dumped it on the brush. I used only sand-clay fill because "junk" is too big and rough to be moved with a shovel. I told my helpers how much fill to put where, then I shaped it with a rake. Next, my helpers dumped about nine inches of unscreened loam on top of the fill and I smoothed this out, too. These handmade berms totalled about two hundred and fifty feet long, were between two and ten feet high, and averaged about four feet high.

Some of my berms are not quite as natural-looking as they should be—they're a bit too straight, a little too even along the top, and steeper than they should be.

However, the large berms on or near the street are steep because I had to make them as high as possible (to provide as much screening as possible) while fitting them into narrow spaces. If the berm along the driveway were any wider it would spill onto my neighbor's property. If the berm along the street were any wider it would cover the bases of some giant white pines and may well have killed them by now. I softened the steep slopes of both berms by planting them with lots of shrubs.

At least one of the larger berms in the woods is steeper than it should be on one side because making it wider might have harmed some white pines. (Like all the trees in Evergreen, they're indispensible in screening the garden from neighboring houses.) Also, a wider berm would have required an enormous amount of dirt, all carried in wheelbarrows, through several hundred feet of woods. Instead of fill, I widened the berm with a thick layer of leaves, which are easier to carry than dirt and less harmful to the pines. Then I softened and partly camouflaged the slope with shrubs.

The brush collected near the brook—including the tons of pine logs and branches dumped at the bottom of the cliffs—was used to build a berm on the southeastern edge of the garden.

This site was farther from the driveway than any other place on the property. Carrying dirt to the site in wheelbarrows would have been a long, hard job so I decided to build the berm with only a little dirt.

We began by making a tight pile of pine logs, extending from the southern end of the cliffs to the edge of the stream. We piled branches on top of the logs, then layered rotted tree matter on top of the branches and dumped several hundred bags of leaves (mostly raked and donated by my neighbors) on top of that. Finally, we added just a few wheelbarrows of loam. When we were done, we had made a six-foot-high, thirty-six-foot-long berm built almost entirely out of tree waste.

The loam, combined with the decaying leaves, made a fine growing medium.

Jewelweed (*Impatiens capensis*), which had been growing along the stream, migrated to the berm and covered it with its delicate light green foliage.

Cleaning up this part of Evergreen was wonderfully economical. It accomplished four things at once:

- It opened up the brook.
- It exposed many square yards of handsome, sheer cliffs on the east side of the brook.
- With the pine tree debris gone, it allowed solid drifts of jewelweed to carpet the slope between the brook and the near-vertical cliffs in the southeast corner of the garden.
- And, of course, it added a beautiful berm.

In other words, the brook and the cliffs didn't have to be made and the jewelweed didn't have to be planted. They were all gifts of the landscape. The brook and the cliffs simply had to be unwrapped. The jewelweed needed only a place to grow. And the berm was made by dropping debris and adding a little loam. Not bad for just a few days' work! Gardening by subtraction doesn't get any better than this.

WATER IN THE WOODLAND GARDEN — STREAMS, POOLS, PONDS, AND WATERFALLS

Nearly every great garden has at least some water—a fountain, a pool, a pond, a stream, a waterfall—and the reason for this is obvious: water is simply the most engaging element in the garden. It offers, paradoxically, both excitement and repose at the same time. In an often static site, it provides motion, both visual and physical. In a garden that's often brown and green, its ripples and cascades offer glistening shades of white; when its smooth surface mirrors the sky, it brings the blues and grays and whites of clouds to the woodland floor. Water may be the strongest focal point and the most interesting accent in an entire garden. And its many sounds—from lapping, to trickling, to shushing, to splashing, to wild surging—add aural excitement to an otherwise quiet place. If you have water in your garden, you may give it more attention than anything else there.

Some residential woodlands already have water—a stream or even a small pond. If your stream is a large, lively brook, cascading beautifully over rocks or even featuring at least one long, white glistening waterfall, it is already a dazzling water feature. You'll probably have to do next to nothing to improve it.

Small, quiet, sometimes seasonal, brooks, with only a few tiny cascades may be easily enhanced by a manmade but natural-looking pool or cascade.

Big or small, improved or not, any naturally running water in a garden is a literally priceless asset.

ENHANCING AN EXISTING STREAM

If you already have a stream—whether it's a tepid streamlet or a torrent pouring over a little Niagara Falls—you can enhance it in the same way you can improve the rest of your woods: by cleaning up and weeding both the stream bed and the land around it, by building paths that provide good views of the brook, by planting appropriate shrubs and flowers, and perhaps by adding furniture and sculpture.

To create as many views of your pond or stream as possible, try to make a path along its entire length. To maximize your enjoyment of the water, put the path as close to it as you can.

If you need to use fill to make the path, make sure you put it above the high-water mark to avoid erosion damage. You can also help protect the fill by placing rocks between it and the water. Don't use too many rocks, though, or they won't look natural—they'll look like what they are: a manmade retaining wall.

MAKING STONE CROSSINGS, PIERS, AND CAUSEWAYS

If you have a stream in your woods, you'll probably want to be able to cross it, not just to reach the other side but so you can stand above the middle of the brook and have a long, water-filled view of the stream.

One way to cross a stream, of course, is over a bridge. Some bridges are both practical and beautiful. Stone or wooden arched bridges or Chinese moon bridges, for example, are all picturesque accents.

Attractive bridges, however, are costly. Stone structures require concrete abutments and foundations as well as skilled stone masonry. If the brook isn't accessible to trucks and other equipment, the sand, cement, and stones needed to build the bridge will have to be carried to the site by hand and the concrete will have to be mixed in a portable mixer—just a couple of reasons why even small stone bridges cost at least several thousand dollars apiece and why larger structures can run into five figures.

Wooden bridges are much less expensive. Smaller spans—which can be bought premade at garden supply stores—cost only a few hundred dollars. Like all outdoor wooden structures, however, wooden bridges need annual maintenance and eventually wear out anyway. Over time, the cost of repairing and replacing wood bridges approaches the cost of building a stone bridge.

Both wooden and stone bridges have yet another disadvantage: although they can be attractive, they can never look truly natural. Put any bridge across a stream,

Opposite: A brook splashes over mossy green rocks at Evergreen.

and the purely natural character of the place is lost.

Stones, stone piers, and causeways are three natural and highly economical alternatives to bridges.

If a stream is shallow and gently flowing, you may be able to cross it on a row of large, flat-topped rocks. For stability—and to make the rocks look as natural as possible—use the largest stones you can find and make sure they're well seated in the stream bed. You can also make the rocks look natural by choosing stones from the site, using differ-

ent sized stones, arranging them in an irregular, jagged curve—never in a straight line—and placing them at unequal distances from each other (see figures 7 and 8). Be sure to set them close enough so you can walk across them easily.

Piers are another alternative to bridges. Made of rocks, fill, and loam, piers are little points or peninsulas extending into the stream. They're built similar to causeways. If a stream is small and slow moving—and many are—you can build a pier almost all the way across it. (The water will flow

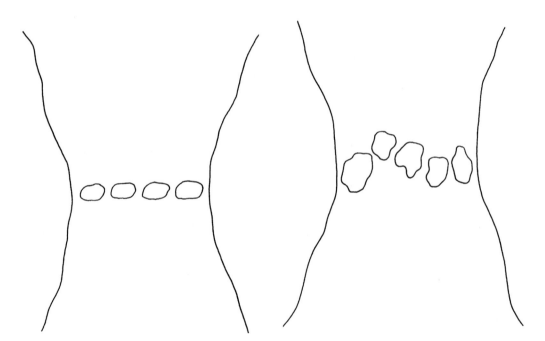

FIGURE 7: *When placing rocks in a stream so you can walk across it, don't use rocks of similar size or shape and don't place them in a straight line, equidistant from each other. . .*

FIGURE 8: *. . . instead, make the rocks look natural by using stones of different sizes and shapes, arranging them in an irregular, jagged curve, and varying the distances between them.*

through the narrow channel between the pier and the opposite bank.) You cross the stream by walking to the end of the pier, then stepping across the channel to the other side (see figure 9).

You can also build two piers, one on each side of the brook, that approach each other in the stream. To cross the brook, you walk to the end of one pier, then step across the narrow channel separating the ends of the piers (see figure 10).

Piers will work only if the stream is small enough to flow freely through a channel narrow enough to step across easily—no more than eighteen inches wide.

If the stream needs more space to flow, you may be able to combine a pier or piers with one or more large rocks. Build one or two piers into the stream, leaving a wide

channel between them. Then place large rocks in the channel, as explained above. Instead of stepping across the channel, you cross it on the rocks.

If the stream is too large to cross with piers (or piers and rocks), you can build a causeway. Like piers, causeways are long piles of rocks covered with fill and loam. Unlike piers, however, causeways go all the way across the stream. One or more pipes are placed inside them to let the water flow through the structure.

Building a causeway is simple, do-it-yourself work. First, determine its dimensions. A causeway should be high enough to remain above water level even when the stream is flowing at its fullest. The top of the causeway should be at least two feet wide for easy walking.

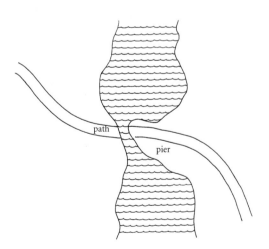

FIGURE 9: *Small streams can be crossed by building a pier on one bank . . .*

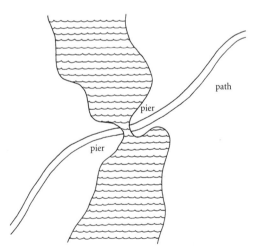

FIGURE 10: *. . . or on both banks.*

To determine how long the pipes under the causeway should be, you'll also have to estimate the width of the bottom of the causeway. A handy rule of thumb is that, when rocks are dumped in a pile, the slope of the pile (known as the "angle of repose") will be about forty-five degrees from the ground. A pile with a forty-five-degree angle of repose will have about two feet of width at the bottom for every foot of height. To put it another way, the width of the bottom of the pile will be the same as the width of the top of the pile plus about two feet for every foot of height. A two-foot-high causeway that's three feet wide at the top, for example, will be about seven feet wide at the base (four feet for the two feet of height plus three feet for the three feet of width at the top). Because pipes should be long enough to span the bottom of the causeway, but not long enough to stick out and be seen, they should be about as long as the bottom of the causeway is wide.

Next, determine the number and diameter of the pipes. If you want all the water in the stream always to flow through the pipes, the total area of the cross sections of the pipes should be at least as large as the total area of the cross section of the stream when the stream is flowing at its fullest. To compute the total area of the pipes, multiply the square of the radius of each pipe by 3.141 (pi) and add up the areas of all the pipes. To compute the area of a cross section of the stream, multiply its average fullest depth at one point by its width at the same point.

To build the causeway, dump a layer of rocks on the stream bed and lay the pipes on top of them, parallel to the banks. Pile stones on top of the pipes, from one side of the brook to the other. Cover the protruding ends of the pipes with stones to disguise them. To make the causeway look natural, give it an irregular shape like a berm. Make it curving, not straight; make it slightly wider in some places than others; make some of the slopes longer (and gentler) than the others; and make the top of the causeway slightly sloping, not level.

Cover the rocks with fill, and work the dirt into the crevices by raking it back and forth, tamping, and wetting it. Pack down the fill on top of the causeway to make a hard, smooth path. Then cover the path and any other visible fill with a layer of loam, so the surface of the causeway is the same color as the rest of the paths. If the slopes of the causeway are wide and gentle enough, you might plant them with an evergreen ground cover (see figure 11).

Because most of the water will flow through the pipes, erosion damage should be slight. If some causeway dirt washes away, simply replace it. You can minimize erosion by making the slopes of the causeway as gentle as possible and by adding ground covers or other plants to the above-water portions to stabilize them.

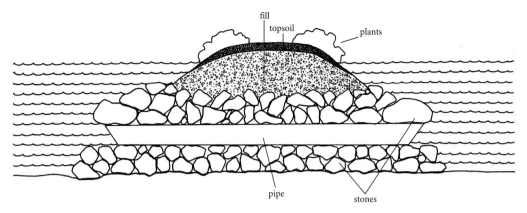

FIGURE 11: *To build a casueway, dump rocks on the bottom of the stream, lay pipes, and add more stones. Then cover the stones with fill and a layer of topsoil and add plants.*

MAKING WATERFALLS

Waterfalls are nature's fountains. They are among the liveliest, most arresting, and most beautiful water features. If you have a stream in your woods, one of the best ways to enhance it is to create one or more falls.

To make a true fall, you must make your stream drop through the air. To make the fall as impressive as possible, make it fall as far as possible and make it as large as you can by channelling all of your stream, or as much of it as you can, into the fall.

The easiest way to make water fall is to channel it over a large, flat, cantilevered (overhanging) rock or rocks. If you have a suitable rock, but your stream flows around it, you may be able to channel the water over it with a dike, which is a damlike structure made of rocks or fill, sandbags covered with rocks or fill, or both. Simply build the dike high enough and thick enough to con-

trol the water and make it go where you want it to. As with causeways and dams, make the dike look as natural as possible.

First, select a good site for a fall—ideally, one with a narrow channel to concentrate the water above the rock and a long drop below it.

If the stream doesn't channel the water naturally—and most stream beds don't—you'll have to build one or more dikes on either side of the flow to force it into a narrow path. You can make the water fall farther by digging away the stream bed beneath the fall. Be careful not to dig up too much of the bed or you may make the rocks above it unstable, or the stream may leak through the bed underneath the rocks instead of flowing over them.

If you don't already have rocks suitable for a fall in your stream bed, you can install them. You may find large flat rocks suitable for a fall on your land or you may be able to gather them (with permission) on a neighbor's property. They're also sold at masonry suppliers or quarries.

MAKING POOLS AND PONDS

Still another way to enhance your stream is by building pools or ponds. (A pond is simply a sheet of water that's too big to be called a pool.) Pools and ponds do many things a brook usually can't:

- ☙ Their smooth surfaces constantly mirror the many colors of the sky.
- ☙ Usually wider than streams, often more impressive and more dramatic, a pool or pond's mirror images are also much larger.
- ☙ Unlike a running brook, the still water of a pool can support aquatic plants such as waterlilies, and it makes a comfortable home for goldfish and frogs.

To make a pool, you'll need a dam. Like cleaning up, weeding, pruning, and grading, building small dams is simple but exhilarating do-it-yourself work.

You can build a relatively watertight dam with nothing more than sand-clay fill in plastic sandbags. (Make sure the bags are plastic, not burlap or other organic material, which will rot. Plastic, on the other hand, will last indefinitely if kept out of the sun—one of the few virtues of non-biodegradability.)

To build a dam, simply fill the bags about half full, fold the ends of the bags under the sacks, and place them, ends down, in a row across the stream bed. Make sure the fold is facing upstream (see figure 12). The weight of the sandbag will hold the folded ends in place. To make the dam as watertight as possible, push the sandbags as close to each other as you can.

To make the dam higher, lay another row of bags on top of the first. To make the dam as strong and watertight as possible, "bond" the bags by placing them so the centers of the bags in the top row are above the joints, or places where the sides of the bags touch, in the row below. Keep adding rows until the dam is as high as you want it.

For low dams—one foot high or less—one "wall" of sandbags is usually sturdy enough. For higher dams, build two or more "walls," placed tightly against each other.

To make the dam look natural, finish it the way you would a causeway (explained earlier): cover its upstream and downstream sides with stones, cover the stones with fill, and cover the fill with loam. The wider and more irregular you make the rock-fill-and-loam covering, the more natural it will look and the stronger the dam will be.

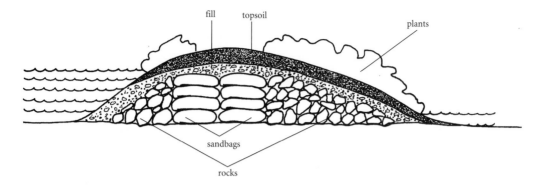

fill topsoil plants

sandbags

rocks

FIGURE 12: *To build a dam, build one or more walls of sandbags across a stream and dump rocks above and below the bags. Cover everything with layers of fill and topsoil and add plants.*

You'll also have to build a spillway, or channel, for excess water to run over the dam. To minimize erosion damage, line the channel with rocks.

Rocks, fill, and sandbags are not the only things needed to make a pool—as I quickly discovered many years ago. One day I carefully laid sandbags across my brook and watched joyfully as the water swiftly rose higher and higher. By the time I laid the last sandbag I had created a room-size pool, spilling over the top of my newly made dam. I was euphoric.

The next morning the water was gone.

I figured out that, to fill a pool, the volume of water in a stream must be larger than the volume escaping through the dam or through the bottom or sides of the pool. When I built the pool, my brook was flowing unusually full—it contained more than enough water to replace the water leaking

through the dam and the pool bed. The next morning the brook was flowing much more slowly, and every bit of water flowing into the pool was flowing right out of it.

It's impossible to tell in advance merely by looking if water will stay in a newly dammed pool or not. But there are some clues to watch out for: water seeps faster out of a sandy, rocky, or ledgy streambed than out of a bed with a lot of clay. And, obviously, a large, fast-flowing stream replaces lost water faster than a small, sluggish one.

The only way to know for sure if a pool will stay full is to start building it. While the stream is flowing slowly, build a small, low dam by laying a row of sandbags across the bed. If the pool fills up to the height of the bags, you'll know that even a slow-flowing stream has enough water to keep the pool full—at least to this height. If you want to see how much water the pool will hold, build the dam higher. Stop building when either the pool is as full as you want it, or it won't hold any more water.

Unfortunately, some small streams, like mine, are only seasonal: in late summer or during dry weather, they disappear. Needless to say, any pools along these streams will disappear as well. The erstwhile pools will hold only mud, not water, and mud is not attractive. If you have a seasonal brook and want to build a pool, you'll have to decide whether a possibly unsightly pool in dry weather is worth a lovely pool in wet weather.

Seasonal pools also can't support perennial waterlilies or other water plants, and goldfish and frogs can't live in them year-round. Their main asset is simply water.

It's possible to create a year-round pool in a seasonal brook by lining the stream bed with concrete and adding water to the pool with a hose in dry weather. Such projects, however, are neither cheap nor foolproof. In cold climates, the bed must be dug deeply so you can build footings below the frostline. Otherwise, the concrete will probably shift and crack in cold weather. If the brook is inaccessible to a backhoe or other power equipment, the bed will have to be dug with a pick and shovel. Also, the sand and cement will have to be carried to the brook by hand, and the concrete will have to be made in a portable mixer. Furthermore, the pool will almost inevitably develop cracks and they'll

have to be patched. Unlike a sandbag dam, which can be made with as little as fifty dollars' worth of fill and sandbags, a concrete pool can cost several thousand dollars to build, plus more money to maintain.

Another alternative is Bentonite, a special clay that can create a virtually watertight seal on the bottom of a pond. Bentonite is usually cheaper than concrete and, unlike concrete, it won't crack. On the other hand, Bentonite is soft, so it must be protected from erosion and other disturbances. And, like concrete, it requires expert installation to be effective.

At the other extreme from seasonal brooks are streams that flow so full and fast all year round they can easily fill a pool with only a fraction of their water. Dams on these streams hardly have to be watertight. You can forget about sand bags and build them as you would a causeway: with rocks covered with fill. In fact, if the volume of water is especially large, you may have to install pipes under the dam to help carry the excess water away. (If the volume of water declines during dry periods, simply block up one or more of the pipes.)

Opposite: Goldfish swim beneath the watchful eyes of the Virgin Mary in a lily pool at Evergreen. The pool is surrounded by vinca, red and pink impatiens, and masses of rhododendrons.

The essential difference between a dam and a causeway, after all, isn't how they're made but what they do: dams impound water; causeways allow you to cross water (and enjoy views of it). But you can also cross a stream on a dam and a causeway can also hold water (just block the pipes underneath it). In fact, because a garden is usually enhanced by more, not fewer, pools and crossings, your dams and causeways should often do double duty.

Where exactly should you make pools (out of either dams or causeways)? Follow the example of civil engineers: build them where you can create the most water for the least effort. The ideal places for dams—the engineer's idea of heaven—are box canyons with long, wide, nearly level bottoms, high walls on both sides, and another high wall downstream with only a narrow slit where the stream flows through. The slit can be plugged with a narrow dam and the long, wide, deep canyon can fill up with a long, wide, deep lake. A little dam, in other words, can make a lot of water; it's the very model of efficiency. The worst place for a dam, on the other hand, is a wide spot in a level valley with almost no walls anywhere. This kind of topography requires an enormous dam just to create an itty-bitty lake.

If you don't have a stream on your property, or if the stream isn't full or fast enough to fill a pool, you can still have standing water in your woods with an artificial but natural-looking pool.

An artificial pool is made by digging a hole in the ground and lining it with either polyethylene, polyvinylchloride (PVC), butyl rubber, concrete, or a preformed fiberglass pool. Although PVC liners last longer than polyethylene ones, and rubber ones last longer than PVC, all three are subject to tears and punctures and none lasts forever. But they are relatively inexpensive. Concrete, on the other hand, is durable but expensive to install. Fiberglass pools cost more than polyethylene, PVC, or rubber, but they're cheaper than concrete, they last indefinitely, and they come as large as twenty feet long, eight feet wide, and two and a half feet deep.

If you plan to install a pool in your woodland garden, remember that waterlilies and other flowering aquatic plants need at least six hours of direct sunlight per day to bloom. If you want a pond for its flowers, put it in a sunny spot. In a shady woodland garden, a pool is usually installed not for flowers but simply for its water. The glistening water can be an accent, a focal point in a garden room, and a dramatic contrast to the plants and sculpture around it.

To maintain the natural character of a woodland garden, keep these points in mind if you install an artificial pool:

- Locate the pool where it would naturally be: in a low spot on the land.
- Choose an irregular, free-form pool, never a square, rectangle, or other formal, geometric shape.
- Install the largest pool possible, because a larger pool almost always looks more natural.
- Hide the lip of the pool by placing large, flat fieldstones around and overhanging its edge. Make the rock edging look natural by using stones from the site (or that look as if they could be from the site). Use the largest flat rocks you can find, for three reasons:
  - The larger the rock, the larger the part that isn't hanging over the edge of the pool, and the more stable the rock is—especially if someone steps on the edge over the pool.
  - Larger rocks tend to look more natural, as if they were there all along.
  - The larger the rocks, the fewer you'll need, and the fewer seams or spaces you'll have between them. The fewer the seams, and the more the rocks look alike, the less the rocks will look like what they really are—a bunch of rocks—and the more they'll look like a ledge. And no rock looks more natural than a ledge. Planting vinca or other creeping evergreen ground cover around the rocks will help hide seams and make the rock look even more like a ledge.
- Don't add a fountain. They look only slightly less natural than a rectangular pool.

MAKING CAUSEWAYS IN EVERGREEN

I wanted to build two crossings for my brook, not only to walk to the other side but also to provide long upstream views of cascading water. I knew these vistas would be among the most dramatic in the entire garden. Instead of just standing beside the brook and seeing a few cascades nearby, I would be able to stand in the middle of the brook, look upstream, and see literally dozens of cascades falling toward me. No other views of the brook would be nearly so full of so much falling water.

I knew I could build or buy two wooden arched bridges to span the brook, but I wanted to avoid the large cost of buying—and, more importantly, maintaining—two sizeable wooden structures. I also preferred a less architectural, more natural solution.

So I built two dirt-and-stone causeways instead of two bridges.

Like the berm made out of debris, the causeways were models of economy. They were made almost entirely out of the twenty or so wheelbarrow loads of small stones cleaned up on the property.

First, I gathered the unwanted rocks into piles. Then, when the brook was barely flowing, one of my helpers loaded them into a wheelbarrow, brought them (downhill) to the stream, and dumped them in two long piles spanning the stream bed. Both piles were about three feet wide—ample to support a path you could walk across easily. Because the brook is small, I didn't need pipes underneath the rocks. I just made small channels for the water to run through.

My helpers covered the rocks with several wheelbarrow loads of fill. I raked and washed the dirt between the rocks; eventually it filled in most of the spaces around the stones.

We added more fill to the top of the causeways, and I raked and tamped it down to make hard, smooth walkways. Next, I spread a thin layer of loam over the fill so the paths across the causeways were virtually the same color as other paths in the garden. When all the earth was in place, the two causeways were nearly solid dams.

The causeways are not maintenance-free. Nearly all the stones stay put, but from time to time I have to replace some washed-out fill with more dirt. But that's less maintenance than wooden bridges require. And it's a small price to pay for structures that cost almost nothing to build.

The lower causeway has another benefit: it dams the brook into a lovely pool—about fifteen feet wide and twenty feet long—that's ringed by handsome, moss-covered boulders and overhung by a graceful (and carefully pruned) witch hazel. The brook enters the pool in a series of charming cascades. The causeway not only creates the pool, it also provides the perfect place to view both it and the dozens of little waterfalls above it. As you'll see in Part Two, I also installed two fiberglass fishponds on the north side of the house.

PLANTING

After your woods have been cleaned up, weeded, and pruned, they'll be more open, more expansive, and more parklike. Although you won't have added a single plant—in fact, you'll only have taken plants away—your woods will already be much more beautiful than they were when you began.

Still, they'll be a bit bare, containing large trees and little else. There may be an evergreen tree or shrub, some woodland perennials, and maybe a few patches of ground cover here and there, but these smaller plants are like the few odd pieces of furniture left behind when someone moves out of a house. Except for them, your outdoor rooms will be empty. Your woods will need the natural furniture of shrubs and perennials and the natural carpeting of ground covers and low plants.

Like a flower border, your new plantings should be arranged roughly in layers—shortest in front, tallest in back, each plant higher than those in front of it. Plant ground covers and other low plants along paths and in other places on the floor of the garden where they can be most easily seen and where colorful blossoms can have their greatest impact. Put larger flowering plants and smaller shrubs behind the low plants, and place the largest shrubs in the rear where, with the trunks of the trees, they'll help form the walls of the outdoor rooms. For simplicity, I divide all plants into three layers—low, middle, and upper. Together, they sweep up from the floor to the walls of the garden, knitting all elements into a visual whole.

Garden books list literally hundreds of varieties of shade-tolerant plants for woodland gardens, many with beautiful flowers that provide much-welcomed color. Unfortunately, most of these plants are deciduous shrubs and perennial and annual flowers; for all their color and beauty, they're part-time plants. Deciduous shrubs and perennials bloom for only a few weeks each year, and their foliage dies back in the fall, not appearing again until spring. Annuals bloom all summer, but in most of the country they can't be planted until spring and they die in the fall.

If a garden contains only part-time plants, it's a part-time garden: green for just a few months (and colorful for even fewer) and bare for as much as half the year. In cold, northern climates the garden might be bare from when the snow melts in March until the perennials come up in May; bare again from when plants start dying off in September until it snows in December or January; and, of course, bare during mid-winter thaws.

To avoid the bare ground of a part-time garden, use herbaceous perennials and deciduous shrubs sparingly. Instead, plant at least fifty percent of your garden—preferably more—with evergreens.

To make your garden as colorful as possible don't choose shrubs and perennials just for their flowers, which bloom for only a few weeks, but for their colorful foliage, which in deciduous or herbaceous plants lasts all summer long and in evergreen plants lasts all year. And don't use only plants that flower in mid-spring, when most species bloom. Instead, try to have flowers in your garden all season long by using plants that bloom in early spring, summer, and fall as well.

EVERGREEN PLANTS

Unlike shade-tolerant herbaceous plants, of which there are literally hundreds of species, hardy shade-tolerant evergreen species are relatively few—so few that most of the popular genera can be listed here. This relatively small palette of evergreens, however, is not a problem. Most species—mainly shrubs and ground covers—are handsome; there are more than enough for variety; many are variegated so they can provide a welcome touch of white or yellow in a garden of mainly green foliage; and many of the shrubs (especially rhododendrons) have bright, colorful flowers. And if planted in their proper habitat, most evergreens need little care.

BROADLEAVED EVERGREEN SHRUBS

Most broadleaved evergreen shrubs prefer shady locations and cool, moist, rich, slightly acidic soils—exactly the conditions of most woodlands in the United States. Most, however, flower profusely in light, not heavy shade, and for only a few weeks each year (usually spring or early summer). That's why broadleaved evergreen shrubs should be appreciated for their handsome foliage as much as for their flowers. This is especially true in woodland gardens, where shade may be heavy.

Among the shade-loving evergreen shrubs suitable for a woodland garden, perhaps the most valuable in cold-winter climates (which includes most of the Midwest and the Northeast) are rhododendrons (*Rhododendron* spp.). Rhodies are distinguished by their long, smooth, leathery, dark green oval leaves, among the largest of any broadleaved evergreen shrub. Not all rhododendrons, incidentally, are large, shade-loving plants with big leaves. Some species, such as the justly popular P.J.M. (*Rhododendron* 'P.J.M.'), prefer full sun. Other species (many of which are found in warm-winter climates such as the Pacific Northwest) are low, nearly prostrate plants with tiny boxwoodlike leaves.

Rhododendrons also have some of the biggest flower clusters of any broadleaved evergreen shrubs—tight, rounded bouquets known as trusses as large as ten inches wide in some species. Rhodies are available in a large number of flower colors: many different shades of white, red, pink, purple, lavender, mauve, yellow, and orange. In cold-winter climates, most rhodies grow to four to six feet tall, a good height for middle- and upper-layer plantings. In warmer regions, rhododendrons may reach twenty feet. In any climate, their large size, large leaves, dense growth, and stunning

The pink blossoms of the treelike, fourteen-foot-high Rhododendron argyrophyllum. *Nankingense 'Chinese Silver' brightens the woods at the Rhododendron Species Botanical Garden. The tree on the left is a Western hemlock.*

flowers give them a presence matched by few other evergreens.

Most rhododendrons bloom in May (in cold-winter climates). A few bloom as early as April. One of them, 'Cunningham's White' (*R. catawbiense* 'Cunningham'), has white trusses and grows to about four feet, making it a good medium-layer shrub; it's hardy to Zone 4. Another early bloomer, the compact 'Cloudland' (*R. impeditum*), has small leaves and bluish-purple flowers. It grows close to the ground, making it a fine lower-level plant; like many rhododendrons, it's hardy to Zone 5. Both shrubs provide welcome early-spring color.

On the other hand, 'Roseum Elegans' (*R. catawbiense* 'Roseum Elegans') produces its rose-pink flowers in late May and early June (in cold climates), after many other shrubs have already bloomed. Hardy to Zone 4, this vigorous, fast-growing shrub is an excellent screening plant with a mature size of eight feet in height and ten feet in width.

Other Catawba rhododendrons (*R. catawbiense* spp.) grow to about six feet tall (in cold regions), so they also make good upper-layer and screening shrubs. 'White Catawba' (*R. c.* 'Album') has white flowers; 'Elegans Catawba' (*R. c.* 'Album

Opposite: A pink camellia under an ancient live oak, draped with Spanish moss, along the Main Walk at Maclay Gardens.

Elegans') has blush-colored blossoms; 'English Roseum' (*R. c.* 'English Roseum') produces pink flowers in late May; 'Everest' (*R. c.* Everestianum) has rosy-lilac blooms with frilly edges; and the popular 'Nova Zembla' (*R. c.* 'Nova Zembla'), has dark red blossoms and glossy leaves. All are hardy to Zone 4.

One of the largest rhododendrons, the giant rosebay (*R. maximum*), is an especially valuable plant. It can grow more than twenty feet high in warm-winter climates (twelve in colder regions), so it's an ideal screening and upper-layer plant. It's one of the few rhodies hardy to Zone 3, so it can be used virtually anywhere in the northern United States. And it's the only winter-hardy rhododendron that will bloom in deep shade. No wonder it's probably the single most valuable shrub in the Northern woodland garden.

There are literally thousands of other species and varieties of rhododendrons but the differences among many of them are not large (at least to untrained eyes), and most nurseries and garden stores carry only a fraction of them anyway. As with any plant genus, first check to see which grow well in your region. Out of that group, select plants for specific needs (screening, middle- or upper-layer height, sunny or shady location, color, etc.). Narrow your selection further by picking out plants whose blossoms, leaves, etc., you like the best.

Most rhodies grow thickest and bloom most prolifically in light shade. They'll get leggier and bloom less as the shade deepens. (Pruning will increase density but, alas, not flowering.) Their only flaw is a tendency to curl their leaves into unattractive, tight little spirals during subfreezing weather. Once established in a proper habitat, rhodies require virtually no care. Some aficionados, in fact, insist they thrive on neglect. I find that adding a little fertilizer helps them grow faster and maybe bloom a bit more profusely. In sunnier spots, a little extra organic mulch helps keep their soil cool and moist.

Azaleas are a variety of rhododendron, and they like the same growing conditions rhododendrons do. Azaleas, however, have more limited uses. Only some are evergreen, and then only in Zone 5 or warmer climates. Evergreen azaleas are usually smaller than rhododendrons and their leaves are smaller, too, so they lack a rhododendron's remarkable presence when they're not in bloom. They're valuable mainly for their lavish spring flowers, which almost cover the entire bush. Unfortunately, this profuse flowering requires sunlight. In medium or deep shade, most evergreen azaleas won't flower at all, so they should be used mainly for accent or variety, and then only in sunnier places. Depending on their height (usually less than three or four feet), they're best used in the middle layer.

The most valuable evergreen azaleas are those that create color not only with their flowers but also with their fall or winter foliage. 'Delaware Valley White' (R. 'Delaware Valley White'), for example, has white springtime flowers and brilliant yellow fall foliage. 'Hino-Crimson' has brilliant red spring blossoms and dark red fall foliage. 'Mother's Day' produces showy red flowers and has reddish winter foliage. 'Stewartstonian' has bright red blossoms and wine-red winter leaves. Like most evergreen azaleas, these varieties are all hardy to Zone 5 and bloom in May.

There are far more deciduous azaleas than evergreen ones, and they have an even greater variety of flower and fall and winter foliage colors. More importantly, they bloom as early as March and as late as July. For more information see the section on deciduous shrubs.

Like rhododendrons, mountain laurel (*Kalmia latifolia*) is a large shrub, growing as much as eight feet high in northern states. Like azaleas and most other broadleaf evergreen shrubs, however, mountain laurel has relatively small leaves and tends to become open and leggy as it matures, therefore lacking a rhododendron's presence. With enough sunlight, however, it produces exquisite, delicate, pink-and-white flowers and these dazzling blooms make the shrub irresistible. Mountain laurel also has a dozen or so hybrids with striking red or pink flowers. It is best used for variety, especially in sunny spots or light shade. For greatest impact, plant it *en masse* and close together. Occasional deep pruning will help it grow fuller. Mountain laurel is a middle- or upper-layer shrub hardy to Zone 4 and requires care similar to rhododendrons— almost none.

Sheep laurel (*K. angustifolia*), also known as lambkill, is a low, small-leaved shrub that likes moisture. It's valuable because it's hardy to Zone 2 and because it blooms in June and July—later than most shrubs. Its rich lavender-rose flowers resemble mountain laurel's in shape. The variety 'Candida' has white flowers, 'Hammonasset' has blue-rose blossoms, 'Kennebago' dark pink flowers, and 'Poke Logan' light pink. Unlike mountain laurel, sheep laurel does best in full sun.

Japanese andromeda (*Pieris japonica*) is known for its showy hanging clusters of pink or white lily-of-the-valley-like flowers in early to mid-spring, as well as for its uniquely shiny, dark green, pointed, wavy leaves and its reddish new foliage.

Japanese andromeda has several interesting varieties. The leaves of crisp-leaf andromeda (*P. j.* 'Crispa') have especially wavy margins. 'Mountain Fire' and 'Forest Flame' have bright red new foliage. 'Mountain Fire' has another bonus: it blooms especially early—in March or April. Several other varieties, including 'Dorothy Wycoff,' 'Flamingo,' 'Valley Rose,' and 'Wada'

have pink flowers. 'Dorothy Wycoff' also has deep pink buds and wine-red foliage in the winter. All Japanese andromedas are hardy to Zone 5 and, depending on the variety, grow six to twelve feet high.

Chinese andromeda (*P. forrestii*) is similar to Japanese andromeda, but it grows taller—ten feet or more—and has larger leaves. It is hardy to Zone 7.

Dense, wide-spreading 'Brouwer's Beauty' has yellowish-green new foliage and showy deep purple-red flower buds in winter and early spring. Hardy to Zone 5, it grows to about five feet tall and five feet wide.

Mountain andromeda (*P. floribunda*) has prominent pale white buds in winter and early spring and upright (not pendulous) clusters of fragrant white blossoms in mid-spring. It's hardy to Zone 4, but its foliage isn't as interesting or as colorful as Japanese andromeda.

Andromedas need light or medium shade, so they should be planted only in relatively sunny places in the woodland garden. Although they grow to be large shrubs, they should be set out where their special leaves and tiny flowers can be appreciated— relatively close to a path or other observation point.

Like andromeda, leucothoe produces clusters of tiny, white flowers that resemble lily-of-the-valley and its foliage changes with the seasons. Unlike most broadleaved evergreens, leucothoe is low-growing—seldom more than two or three feet high—and its long, narrow, pointed leaves, each one shaped like a miniature trowel, are usually more impressive than its tiny flowers. Among the most colorful varieties is 'Girard's Rainbow' (*Leucothoe fontanesiana* 'Girard's Rainbow'), with new leaves a variegated rainbow of cream, red, and pink. 'Nana' is a dwarf with variegated white and green leaves. The foliage of 'Scarletta' is a rich scarlet in spring, dark green in summer, and shades of burgundy in winter. Compact drooping leucothoe (*L. f.* 'Compacta') has bright burgundy winter foliage, as well as fragrant flowers. All these varieties grow no higher than two feet, except for 'Girard's Rainbow,' which can reach three or four feet. All are hardy to Zone 5, except for compact drooping leucothoe, which will survive in Zone 4.

Leucothoe enjoys deep shade, so it's at home almost anywhere in the woods. It usually grows twice as wide as its height, making it a fine high ground cover, as well as a dependable low- or middle-layer shrub. Unlike most other evergreen shrubs, leucothoe's randomly arching branches sometimes look a little unkempt. For best effect, plant it close together, in masses, and trim off longer shoots if you like.

Two of the most valuable woodland garden shrubs are white-variegated *Euonymus fortunei* 'Emerald Gaiety' and the yellow-variegated *E. f.* 'Emerald 'n Gold.' One of several varieties of wintercreepers, they are especially welcome because they offer year-round color, even in deep shade. They also climb, vinelike, up rocks and trees; but unlike other vines, such as ivy, they won't smother a tree. If they have nothing to climb, both shrubs will spread out, typically five or six feet wide and rarely more than two or three feet high. Like leucothoe, they're excellent middle- or low-layer shrubs or high ground covers. They require virtually no care and are hardy to Zone 4. Sarcoxie wintercreeper (*E. f.* 'Sarcoxie') and Manhattan euonymus (*E. kiautschovica* 'Manhattan') are much less useful because they're not variegated.

Another interesting shrub is Oregon grape (*Mahonia aquifolium*). Its lustrous, dark-green, holly-like leaves turn bronze-purple in winter, and its showy bright yellow flowers turn into grapelike clusters of edible blue-black berries that taste a bit like currants. Oregon grape grows between three and five feet tall and is hardy to Zone 5.

Another West Coast plant—one not widely available in the East—is salal (*Gaultheria shallon*). It's known for its rich green, leathery, five-inch-long leaves and small, scarlet berries. In the fall some of its leaves turn red, yellow, or bronze. Salal grows as high as five feet in moist, shady places (such as its native Pacific rainforests) but only one or two feet in dry, sunny spots. It's hardy to Zone 5.

If you live in or south of Zone 7 (most of the South or far West), your selection of shade-tolerant evergreen shrubs is larger than for gardeners in cooler regions.

One of them, fragrant daphne, or winter daphne (*Daphne odora*), is named for its small, sweet-smelling, rosy purple flowers that appear in late winter and very early spring. The cultivar 'Alba' has white flowers; 'Aureo-marginata' has yellow-bordered leaves. Fragrant daphne grows slowly to about four feet high. It prefers light shade, and its range is Zones 7 to 9.

Rose daphne (*D. cneorum*) is a dainty, low-growing, spreading shrub that produces bright rose-pink flowers in mid-spring. The variety 'Eximea' has somewhat larger, deep pink flowers; 'Alba' has white flowers, and 'Variegata' has rose-pink flowers with cream-edged leaves. Rose daphne will survive in Zone 4, but it's fully evergreen only as far north as Zone 7. Like fragrant daphne, it prefers light shade.

Viburnums are medium to large shrubs with handsome dark green leaves, showy displays of white spring flowers, and red, blue, or black berries in summer, fall, and winter. Several species are evergreen. Leatherleaf viburnum (*Viburnum rhytidophyllum*) has lustrous, deeply wrinkled leaves, clusters of yellowish white flowers as much as eight inches wide, and red berries that turn black and remain on the bush until early winter (if not eaten by birds). Leatherleaf viburnum will grow as high as fifteen feet and, while hardy to Zone 5, it's reliably evergreen only to Zone 7. David viburnum (*V. davidii*) has large, deeply veined leaves, two- to three-inch-wide clusters of white flowers, and showy blue berries. It grows three to five feet tall in Zones 7 to 9.

Laurustinus (*V. tinus*) has lustrous, almost black leaves, fragrant white flowers in early spring, and metallic blue berries that later turn black. It grows eight to ten feet tall in Zones 7 to 10. 'Eve Price' and 'Spring Bouquet' are compact varieties with smaller leaves and pinkish white flowers. All these viburnums prefer light shade. (Other viburnums are deciduous. See the deciduous shrubs section.)

Unlike viburnums, Japanese aucuba (*Aucuba japonica*) will flourish in even the shadiest woods. Aucuba is valuable not for its inconspicuous flowers but for its large, showy scarlet berries, which appear in the fall and remain on the plant through the winter, and especially for its handsome variegated leaves, which provide year-round color. The variety 'Crotonifolia' has white spots on green leaves, 'Picturata' has a large splotch of yellow in the middle of each of its spotted green leaves, and the celebrated 'Variegata' (also known as the Gold Dust plant) has lovely gold-flecked green leaves. Like mountain laurel, aucuba is a large shrub that becomes leggy with age. Plant it in the upper layer where its leggy lower stems can be hidden by smaller shrubs in front of it. To have berries, you'll need a female plant (to produce the fruits) and a male plant (to fertilize them). Aucuba's range is Zones 7 to 10.

Like aucuba, the greatest strength of thorny eleagnus, or silverberry (*Eleagnus pungens*), isn't its tiny fragrant white autumn flowers or its red spring berries but the lovely foliage of its variegated varieties. The leaves of 'Variegata' have elegant white or yellow margins and silvery undersides; 'Aurea' has gold-edged foliage; and 'Maculata,' perhaps the most beautiful of all, has golden yellow blotches in the center of each of its leaves. Thorny eleagnus grows quickly to as high as fifteen feet. It prefers light shade but will tolerate much more, and it grows in Zones 7 to 10.

Like other members of the genus, Japanese euonymus (*Euonymus japonica*) is renowned not for its nearly inconspicuous flowers or even its red autumn berries but for the foliage of its variegated varieties. The leaves of 'Silver Knight' have creamy white borders, while the leaves of 'Matanzaki' are edged in golden yellow. Like thorny eleagnus, Japanese euonymus is fast-growing to as high as fifteen feet, and it thrives in Zones 7 to 10.

Another mild-winter shrub is Japanese aralia (*Fatsia japonica*), also known as *Aralia japonica* or *Aralia Sieboldiana*. This impressive bush produces small black berries in fall and large showy clusters of tiny, milky white flowers in fall and winter when practically nothing else is in bloom. It has striking tropical-looking foliage— glossy, dark green, deeply lobed leaves as much as sixteen inches wide. The leaves of 'Variegata' are especially useful because they have either golden or creamy borders. Vigorous and fast-growing, Japanese aralia can quickly reach eight feet in height. Although hardy to Zone 7, it may flower only in Zones 8 to 10.

Fatshedera (*Fatsia japonica x Fatshedera lizei*) is a cross between Japanese aralia and English ivy, with the flower clusters of the shrub and the large, pointed, lobed leaves and vinelike climbing habit of ivy. It grows quickly to six feet high, and its range is Zones 7 to 10.

Sarcococca is known for its tiny but fragrant white flowers and its small, long, waxy, wavy-edged, deep green leaves. Fragrant sarcococca (*Sarcococca ruscifolia*) grows between three and six feet high. Sweet box (*S. hookerana* var. *humilis*) seldom grows higher than two feet. All do well in heavy shade.

An unusually low shrub, *Skimmia reevesiana* rarely grows taller than two feet. It's noted for its four-inch-long, lance-shaped, dark green leaves, small white spring flowers, and red berries that stay on the plant into the winter. Its range is Zones 7 and 8.

Ternstroemia (*Ternstroemia gymnamthera*) is grown not for its small, fragrant yellow flowers but for its lustrous, deep green, three-inch-long leaves. It also grows between four and ten feet high, so it's a fine background or upper-layer shrub.

Mahonia bealei has the prickly, ivylike leaves, yellow flowers, and blue-black berries of its cousin, Oregon grape, but it grows much taller—up to twelve feet—and its range is Zones 7 to 9.

If you live in or south of Zone 8 (most of which is in the Deep South and on the West Coast), you can also grow at least four other beautiful plants, all of which do best in light shade.

Tobira or Japanese pittosporum (*Pittosporum tobira*) has creamy yellow spring flowers that smell like orange blossoms and leathery, lemon-scented, dark-green, paddle-shaped leaves. It can resemble an upright pachysandra. 'Variegatum' is especially attractive because it has cream-edged, gray-green leaves similar to variegated pachysandra. Growing as high as fifteen feet, pittosporum makes a handsome, graceful, treelike plant for the upper layer. At the other extreme, the dense 'Wheeler's Dwarf' grows only three feet high.

Gardenia (*Gardenia jasminoides*) is grown for its shiny, dark green leaves and elegant,

A pink lady's-slipper in bloom at the edge of the patio at Evergreen.

highly fragrant, three- to four-inch-wide pure white flowers that bloom from spring to summer. The varieties 'August Beauty' and 'Veitchii' bloom from spring to fall. All three shrubs grow to between four and six feet tall. Other varieties, such as 'Radicans' and 'Prostrata,' are much smaller. Although gardenias grow in Zones 8 to 10, long periods of frost (likely in Zones 8 and 9) will damage its foliage.

Tall shrubs with dense, glossy foliage, camellias produce large white, pink, or red single, double, or semidouble flowers from fall to spring, providing rare and welcome color during the coldest months of the year. Common camellia or Japanese camellia (*Camellia japonica*) can reach twenty feet tall and blooms from late fall to early spring. The variety 'Kumasaka' has still another virtue: it's variegated. Sasanqua camellia (*C. sasanqua*) grows six to ten feet tall and blooms from early fall to early winter. Because camellias are rather stiff, rigid plants, they're sometimes hard to blend into a naturalistic woodland setting; they usually look best planted *en masse*. Although camellias are hardy to Zone 8, heavy frosts can damage their flowers.

Three other evergreen shrubs that tolerate shade are yews (*Taxus* spp.) and hemlocks, both needle-leaved evergreens, and boxwood (*Buxus* spp.). None have remarkable foliage and none produce notable flowers—two good reasons for using them sparingly as variety or accent, if you use them at all.

EVERGREEN GROUND COVERS

While evergreen shrubs should comprise more than half of the plantings in your medium and upper layers, evergreen ground covers should constitute the majority of the plants in the lower layer. All of them have shiny, leathery dark green leaves and form dense carpets of foliage. Many are also variegated. Like evergreen shrubs, they prefer shady environments and cool, moist, rich, slightly acidic soils.

Pachysandra or Japanese spurge (*Pachysandra terminalis*) is said to be the most popular ground cover in the United States, and it's easy to see why. It will grow even in dense shade (making it suitable for virtually any woodland garden), it's hardy to Zone 4, it roots easily, and it seems to suffer less winter damage than any other ground cover. I've planted thousands of pachysandra seedlings and I can't remember losing more than a handful. Pachysandra is also the least expensive evergreen ground cover. In 1996, a tray of one hundred rooted cuttings cost about thirty dollars at most retail outlets. Planted between six and nine inches apart, one hundred plants will cover about sixteen square feet. In about three years they'll spread by underground rhizomes to form a neat, flat, dark green carpet of foliage that looks handsome all year round. Pachysandra's dense foliage is its own mulch—it helps keep its soil moist and, especially in shade, will suppress almost any other plant that tries to grow beside it.

One variegated variety, 'Silver edge,' is especially attractive. Its leaves are blue-green with creamy white margins. It's less vigorous and more expensive than *Pachysandra terminalis*, but it's useful as a year-round color accent.

Like pachysandra, *vinca minor* (also known as myrtle or periwinkle) grows in all kinds of shade, it's hardy to Zone 4 and roots easily. Unlike pachysandra, its long, vinelike stems are susceptible to winter damage. Vinca is more expensive than pachysandra and, after it's planted, it doesn't fill in as evenly. It has, however, something no other evergreen ground cover has: lovely five-petaled, one-inch-wide, lavender-blue flowers that bloom for several weeks in the spring. Because, like most plants, vinca blossoms more profusely in sun than shade, use it in sunnier spots and leave the cheaper and more vigorous pachysandra for shadier places.

Vinca has several interesting varieties. 'Alba' has white flowers; 'Bowles Variety' has large white flowers; 'Blue myrtle' has blue blossoms; and 'Atropurpurea' has reddish purple flowers. Several varieties have blue flowers and variegated foliage: 'Variegata' has green leaves with creamy edges; 'Aureomarginata' has green leaves with

bright, yellowish edges; 'Aureovariegata' has green leaves with warm yellow blotches; and 'Sterling Silver' has green-and-white leaves.

Ivy (*Hedera* spp.) can be difficult to grow. I've planted many seedlings that simply refused to take; it was as if they were on a hunger strike. Other seedlings developed only at glacial speed. Once established ivy is tenacious. But when pachysandra, vinca, and other ground covers are available, I would be reluctant to invest much time or money on such a moody plant. Also, unlike vinca, ivy seldom produces flowers. Its principal value is the year-round white or yellow leaf color provided by its variegated varieties. If you decide to try ivy, try just a little to see how it works for you and plant a variegated type.

The loveliest variegated ivy—so beautiful that it can tempt you to forgive all its sins—is 'Gold Heart' (*H. helix* 'Gold Heart'), a variety of English ivy named after the large, warm splotch of creamy white in the center of its shiny green leaves. English ivy also has two other green-and-yellow variegated varieties, 'Buttercup' and 'Sulphurea.' A white variegation, 'Glacier,' has green leaves with a thin white edge. Unfortunately, English ivy is reliably hardy only to Zone 6.

Another pretty variegated ivy is *H. colchica* 'Dentato-variegata,' a variety of Persian ivy with bright cream and

The reddish new leaves of Pieris japonica *'Flame of the Forest' and the white blossoms of a dogwood create spring color in the Glen at the Bloedel Reserve.*

gray-green marbling on its large, dark green leaves. Persian ivy, however, is hardy only to Zone 8.

Several low-growing varieties of euonymus, or wintercreeper, make rich-textured ground covers. Purpleleaf wintercreeper (*Euonymus fortunei* 'Colorata') turns shades of deep purple in fall and winter. Several other varieties are variegated: 'Gracilis' has white or yellowish leaves that turn rose-colored in winter, 'Variegata' has bright green and yellow leaves, and the dwarf 'Kewensis' has tiny, white-veined leaves. All are hardy to Zone 5. As with many plants, the newer, more interesting, usually variegated varieties are more expensive and harder to find than the older, more common types. Also, wintercreeper is well named; unlike pachysandra, it grows slowly and unevenly.

European wild ginger (*Asarum europeaum*) is prized not for its inconspicuous flowers but for its unusually glossy, dark green, heart-shaped leaves. It prospers in even the deepest shade, and it's hardy to Zone 5. Unfortunately, it's more expensive and not as vigorous as other ground covers, so use it mainly for variety. Other wild gingers are not as attractive because their leaves aren't as glossy. Wild gingers aren't related to the spice, by the way; they just smell like it.

Often mistaken for ginger is galax (*Galax urceolata*). Galax has similar low, dark green, heart-shaped leaves; it also likes deep shade and is hardy to Zone 5. Its leaves, however, aren't as shiny as ginger's.

DECIDUOUS PLANTS

Shade-tolerant deciduous shrubs and perennial and annual flowers provide only seasonal and often unremarkable foliage. Most blossom well only in light shade. Use them sparingly, for variety or accent.

DECIDUOUS SHRUBS Late-blooming deciduous azaleas (*Rhododendron* spp.) are especially useful in the woodland garden because they're one of the few shade-tolerant shrubs that flower in late June or July. What's more, they're hardy to Zone 4 and their flowers are fragrant. 'Golden Showers' has peachy-yellow flowers in July, and its glossy green leaves turn bronze in fall. 'Innocence' produces fragrant masses of small white blossoms, and its slightly bronzy foliage turns burgundy red in fall. The pale yellow flowers of 'Lemon Drop' have a slight lemon scent; its blue-green foliage turns red in fall. The flowers of 'Lollipop' are pink in mid-June and silver-pink by month's end. 'Parade' has dark pink flowers with an orange eye, and 'Pink 'n Sweet' has pink blossoms with a lighter pink and yellow center. As with all deciduous shrubs, the lighter the shade, the better the flowering.

Equally if not more valuable late-blooming shrubs, are hydrangeas (*Hydrangea* spp.). They are vigorous growers with large, coarse leaves and large white, pink, or blue flowers that bloom for weeks in July, August, and even September when most other shrubs have long gone by.

Big-leaf hydrangeas (*H. macrophylla*), with large six- to ten-inch flower clusters, are especially showy. 'Niko Blue' has big, globe-shaped flower clusters in July and August. 'Pink Beauty' has pink flowers and dark red new stems. 'Red Flower' (*H. m.* 'Alpenguhlen') has reddish purple flowers. The blossoms of Pink Flower Hydrangea (*H. m. serrata* 'Preciosa') are pink at first, then crimson. All these varieties grow four to five feet tall. In contrast, Compact Bigleaf Hydrangea (*H. m.* 'Compacta'), which has blue flowers, grows only two feet tall. Blue Lacecap Hydrangea (*H. m.* 'Coerulea') grows three to six feet tall and produces deep blue flower clusters that resemble a lacy pinwheel. The unusual Variegated Lacecap Hydrangea (*H. m.* 'Variegata') has blue to pink flowers and green leaves with creamy white margins. All big-leaf hydrangeas grow in Zones 5 to 10. (Blue-flowered hydrangeas, incidentally, become pink in less acid soils, and pink-flowered hydrangeas become bluer in more acid soils. To increase soil acidity, add aluminum sulphate tablets; to decrease acidity, add ground limestone.)

Panicle hydrangeas (*H. paniculata*) are taller than big-leaf hydrangeas, reaching fifteen feet. They have even larger flower clusters—sometimes a foot long or longer—and bloom well into September. They're even hardier than big-leaf hydrangeas to Zone 3, but not as colorful. The flowers of the fast-growing P.G. Hydrangea (*H. p.* 'Grandiflora'), for example, are creamy at first, then bronzy-pink, then brown—typical of the species. Blues and pure pinks are not in the palette.

Oakleaf hydrangea (*H. quercifolia*) is named after its oaklike leaves, which turn red or purple in autumn. The shrub also has interesting reddish twigs, exfoliating bark, and white flowers that turn pink or tan later in the summer. The varieties 'Snow Queen' and 'Snowflake' have larger and more numerous flowers. Oakleaf hydrangeas grow four to six feet tall and are hardy to Zone 5.

The species that blooms most prolifically in shade is *Hydrangea arborescens*. Hardy to Zone 3, it has dark green leaves, white flowers, and grows three to five feet tall. The variety 'Hills of Snow' (*H. a.* 'Grandiflora') blooms all summer long.

Deciduous viburnums (*Viburnum* spp.) are less useful than hydrangeas because their typically white blossoms appear in the spring, when flower color can be provided by evergreen plants. If you plant viburnums, choose a variety with profuse or fragrant flowers, brightly colored berries, and colorful fall foliage. One of the showiest varieties is 'Marie's Doublefile' (*V. plicatum tomentosum* 'Mariesii'), distinguished by its elegant rows of large, three- to five-inch-wide white

spring flowers, bright red berries, and reddish-purple autumn foliage. Like many viburnums, it grows eight to ten feet tall and is hardy to Zone 5. Korean spice, or Mayflower viburnum (*V. carlesii*), which grows six to eight feet tall and is hardy to Zone 4, has fragrant white flowers.

Japanese kerria (*Kerria japonica*) is a graceful, arching shrub that produces a profusion of lovely yellow flowers in the spring. *K. japonica* 'Pleniflora' has double flowers that last longer than the single flowers of the species. *K. japonica* 'Aureovariegata' has yellow-edged leaves; *K. japonica* 'Picta' has white-edged leaves. Hardy to Zone 5, kerria will grow with little care to between four and six feet tall.

Glossy abelia (*Abelia grandiflora*) is known for its lovely soft-pink trumpet-shaped flowers, which bloom all summer long. Some of its varieties grow as high as eight feet; others are much lower. The shrub is hardy to Zone 5 and evergreen in warmer climates. Like most shrubs, it flowers best in light shade.

HERBACEOUS PLANTS Because the menu of shade-tolerant perennials and annuals is as long as the list of shade-loving shrubs is short, and because you'll

Opposite: 'Nova Zembla' rhododendrons at the edge of Evergreen's Gold Room.

want relatively few of these nonevergreen plants anyway, you can afford to be picky. Choose plants that really earn their keep. Look for four things:

- Plants well suited to the site. Use them where light, soil, moisture, etc., provide optimum growing conditions.
- Plants that do well in the heavy or deep shade often found in woodland gardens.
- Perennials with interesting foliage. Perennial flowers bloom for just a few weeks; it's their leaves that you'll be looking at all summer long.
- Plants that give you the most color, either with variegated yellow, white, or blue leaves or with many large, colorful or long-lasting flowers.

Remember that the ground where you plant perennials or annuals will be bare much of the year. Use these plants with great restraint.

The following species all do well in the rich, moist, often acidic soil of deeply shaded woods.

Hostas are perhaps the most useful woodland garden perennials. They're tough, hardy to Zone 3, thrive even in deep shade, and their low, thick clusters of large, elegant, gracefully arching leaves give the plants uncommon presence. Most importantly, many varieties have blue, blue-green, white-and-yellow-variegated, or solid-colored leaves that offer a lot of color all season long. So important, in fact, is the foliage that hosta's tiny flowers are virtually afterthoughts.

Hosta undulata 'Albomarginata' is one of several varieties with green and white leaves. *H. Sieboldiana* is a striking blue-green variety. 'Piedmont Gold' and 'Fanfare' both have yellow leaves. Pick your most colorful favorites.

Variegated hostas are best appreciated up close, where the fine bands of colors on their rippled leaves are most easily seen. Plant them in the lower layer, near paths or other viewpoints.

Hostas are a favorite food of snails and slugs. If you notice leaf damage, set small bowls of beer into the earth beside the plants. The beer kills slugs when they slide into it. If you'd rather not bother with filling bowls and emptying dead slugs out of them, use a chemical slug killer.

Other sources of summer-long color are herbaceous ground covers with variegated or striking blue, red, pink or purple foliage.

Variegated goutweed, or bishop's weed (*Aegopodium podagraria* 'Variegatum'), has soft, crinkled, green leaves with white edges. It's hardy to Zone 4 and tolerates deep shade.

Dead nettle (*Lamium maculatum*) is a low, fast-spreading ground cover with small, crinkled, heart-shaped leaves. Like goutweed, it's hardy to Zone 4 and thrives in deep shade. The variety 'Beacon Silver' has striking silver leaves with green edges; 'White Nancy' has silvery green leaves.

Heuchera americana 'Dale's Selection' has attractive purple-blue leaves with deep blue veins and white flowers in early summer. Even better is 'Purple Palace,' with wonderful deep purple leaves that turn bronzy purple in fall. Both plants are hardy to Zone 3.

Lungwort (*Pulmonaria*) also has small, heart-shaped leaves and small blue, white, or pinkish flowers in the spring. The lovely *P. saccharata* 'Mrs. Moon' has pretty silver spots on dark green leaves and small flowers that are pink in bud but blue when open. *P. saccharata* 'Sissinghurst White' has white-spotted foliage and white blossoms. Lungwort is hardy to Zone 4 and grows in deep shade.

Persian epimedium (*Epimedium versi-color* 'Sulphureum') has striking deep red, heart-shaped leaves with prominent green veins, as well as delicate white flowers in the spring. It's hardy to Zone 5 and does well in moderate shade.

Ajuga reptans 'Burgundy Glow' is a rare beauty, with unusual green, white, dark pink, and purple leaves. It's hardy to Zone 3 but, unfortunately, does best in light shade—the darker its setting, the more it tends to wander in search of more light and the more open it becomes.

A much taller source of color is variegated Japanese Solomon's-seal (*Polygonatum odoratum* 'Variegatum'). Like other Solomon's-seals, this variety is impressive: it has long, pointed leaves and can grow as much as two feet tall. Tiny white flowers appear beneath its stems in the spring. Unlike other Solomon's-seals, this one's deep green leaves are edged with striking streaks of yellow. Like lungwort, Japanese Solomon's-seal is hardy to Zone 4 and grows well in deep shade.

Finally, a word about one of the woodland's most popular and most common perennials. Most ferns are not variegated and they don't have flowers, so the only color they add to the garden is green. Nevertheless, their graceful foliage makes them elegant accents in the lower layer. Most ferns are hardy to at least Zone 4. To get the biggest bang for your buck, consider one of the many evergreen varieties.

Most perennial flowers, even so-called "shade-loving" ones, won't bloom—or bloom very well at least—in deep shade. One of the few that will bloom in

The unusual orange-pink blossoms of Rhododendron *'Umpqua chief' x 'Fawn' are set off by a sweep of pachysandra in Hendricks Park Rhododendron Garden.*

moderately deep shade, which means at least some direct sunlight or a lot of indirect light, is foam flower (*Tiarella*), so called because, in the spring, its vertical stalks are covered with delicate-looking clusters of tiny, star-shaped flowers. 'Wherry's Foamflower' (*T. Wherryi*) has the showiest flowers—salmon pink or white. *T. cordifolia* 'Purpurea' has bronzy purple leaves and rose blossoms. Foam flower also has interesting maple-leaflike foliage, and it's hardy to Zone 3.

Another moderate-shade bloomer is Virginia bluebell (*Mertensia virginica*),

known for its tiny, purplish, bell-shaped flowers that bloom in early spring. The plant grows one to two feet high and is hardy to Zone 3. Unfortunately, it dies back totally by mid-summer so, if you plant it, be prepared for scruffy foliage and bare ground.

One of the most impressive shade bloomers is foxglove (*Digitalis*), so called because its large, cup-shaped flowers resemble the ends of the fingers of a glove. In early summer, the flowers almost completely cover the upper portions of its long stalks, creating one of the largest splotches of color in the woodland garden. Technically, most foxgloves are biennials (they live for just two years, blooming in the second), but they self-seed freely so they can be treated like perennials. Foxgloves are between three and five feet tall, making them excellent medium-layer plants. They have either white, pink, purple, red, or yellow flowers, and they're hardy to Zone 4.

Also worth considering are the following diminutive perennials that are native to woodlands and tolerate moderate shade.

Wild sweet william (*Phlox divaricata* 'Mrs. Crockett'), hardy to Zone 4, produces lovely lavender-blue and pale mauve flowers (resembling those of vinca) in the spring.

Christmas rose (*Helleborus niger*), hardy to Zone 4, has white or pink flowers in early spring or late winter.

Oconee bells (*Shortia galicifolia*), hardy to Zone 5, has shiny, galax-like leaves, and white bell-shaped flowers in the spring.

Snow trillium (*Trillium grandiflorum*), also hardy to Zone 5, is known for its ruffs of three oval leaves and its showy three-petaled white, pink, or yellow flowers in mid- to late spring.

Other shade flowers, such as astilbes, bleeding hearts, columbines, etc., are beloved for their blooms but produce those blooms freely only in light, not deep shade. If you plant them in your woods, put them in relatively sunny spots and hope for the best.

Annuals are the most effective way to bring bright color into the woods all summer long. Unlike perennials, however, annuals require frequent watering, so plant only as many as you want to care for and be sure to place them where they'll have the greatest possible effect. Use them sparingly, as accents and focal points. Annuals are to the rest of the garden what a diamond is to a ring.

If hostas are the most valuable woodland perennial, *Impatiens Wallerana* is the most useful annual. It's the only one that produces large numbers of large bright flowers—yellow, orange, white, and many shades of red and pink—in deep shade.

Two other annuals that flourish in deep shade are valuable for their colorful foliage. Coleus is known for its complex multicol-ored scarlet, red, pink, orange, yellow, brown, white, or cream leaves. Varieties with the brightest and simplest foliage can make very showy accents.

Caladiums have large, striking, heart-shaped or arrow-shaped leaves, prominently veined and tinted with different shades of green, white, silver, pink, or red. Unfortunately, caladiums require a hot climate—one where the temperature never falls below seventy degrees.

Other so-called shade-loving annuals—begonias, fuchsias, primulas, etc.—actually love light shade, which is several hours of direct sun per day. In darker places, they bloom only sporadically. Use them only in the sunnier parts of the woodland garden. Remember, unless these plants produce flowers, they're not worth planting.

SITING THE PLANTS

Here are several guidelines to help you decide which plants should go where:

Plant them where they can be best seen. Plants with fine details (small blossoms, delicate foliage, etc.) should be placed near a path or some other observation point where their less conspicuous features can be appreciated. Larger plants should go behind smaller ones.

For screening, use plants large and dense enough to do the job. If year-round screening is needed, use evergreens.

Plant to enhance the topographical features of your garden. When Frederick Law Olmsted and Calvert Vaux built Central Park, they made the relatively flat terrain more interesting by making high places higher and low places lower. You can do the same thing visually. Make hills "higher" by planting large, tall shrubs on their crests and make adjacent valleys "lower" by using mainly low plants in the bottoms.

Create and enhance outdoor rooms. Locate these rooms where the site suggests they should be—for example, in a level spot bordered by high rocks, large trees or steep slopes that already form at least partial walls of the room. Plant tall shrubs at the edge of the "room" to complete the walls. Use low plants on the floor and "furnish" the enclosure with colorful species, including a few especially bright or interesting specimens. You might want to add garden furniture and sculpture for variety and accent.

Plant in large, irregularly shaped sweeps or drifts of the same species. "Drifting" plants accomplishes several things:

- It enhances the natural look of the garden by emulating nature, where plants often appear in large, irregular clusters.
- Large drifts are appropriate to the usually large scale of a woodland garden. They give plants visual strength in numbers and much more presence than they would have in smaller groups.
- Drifting avoids the messy or busy look often resulting when many different kinds of plants are crowded into a small space.

In addition to large drifts, use small clusters and single plants for variety and contrast. The larger and more colorful the plant, the smaller the cluster can be. If the plant is large or colorful enough, a single specimen can stand by itself.

Using just one or a very few bright, blooming plants within a prominent position in a large space of more subdued colors was a favorite trick of Moorish gardeners. They knew that just one colorful plant, needing much less water than a room full of plants, would not be dwarfed by the space but would dominate it and make the entire area look well planted.

Tree roots present a special problem in a woodland garden. They make it almost impossible to dig up the forest floor, and they can make it hard for new plants to take root and survive. Shallow-rooted trees such as pines, maples, and beeches can be especially hard on competing plants. To minimize the problem, try to

Fuchsia azaleas and red camellias in the loblolly pine woodlands of Hodges Gardens.

plant deeper-rooted, water-hungry plants (such as shrubs) as far away from trees as possible without sacrificing the beauty of your design. Try to use tough ground covers like pachysandra or vinca under trees instead.

To help new plants root well, and to make digging much easier, add a layer of loam before you plant. A four- to six-inch layer for ground covers and a $1^1/_2$-foot-high mound for shrubs will allow you to dig in fresh, soft dirt. As with berms, make the mounds look as natural as possible by making them irregularly shaped and gently sloping. The wider the mound, the more protection it will afford the roots of the shrub. Give new plants even more help by amending the soil with peat moss and a little composted manure.

Planting shrubs in mounds has another advantage: it makes the plants look taller. Mounding is one of the best bargains in landscaping: one or two dollars' worth of loam can create as much mass as ten to twenty dollars' worth of shrub.

To suppress weeds and keep the soil cool and moist, spread a layer of organic mulch—leaves, needles, bark mulch, etc.—around each plant. Water new shrubs deeply, with enough water to reach below the roots, twice a week during their first year. With well-mulched soil and deep watering, that's all the water they'll need. If it rains hard on or near a would-be water-ing day, skip watering that day. To make your work easier, use a sprinkler and make sure it runs long enough for plants to get all the water they need (better too long

than too short). If a plant is suited to its site, it should need little if any watering—or much of any other care—after the first year.

PLANTING EVERGREEN

After Evergreen was cleaned up, weeded, and pruned, I was left with an open, almost parklike woodland, as well as a thicker, unweeded woodland bordering the garden that helps screen it from neighboring houses and other development. After I had finished grading and installed water fea-tures, I also had a lovely cascading brook, three pools (one in the brook, two beside my house), and smooth dirt paths that took me easily along the brook and throughout the entire garden. I also had several hundred feet of berms that, even without plantings, already screened out much of the develop-ment in the neighborhood.

Now my garden needed just a little more screening, a lot more plants—shrubs, ground covers, and a few flowers—and some furniture and sculpture.

The need for more screening and shrubs was partly met by 140 rosebay rhododen-drons on or near the tops of most of the berms. The rhododendrons made the berms "higher." I chose rosebays mainly because they're just about the biggest shade-loving broadleaved evergreen shrubs that grow in cold climates. (My garden is in Zone 5.)

What's more, rosebays grow quickly. They were about six feet high when planted, and they'll probably reach twelve feet. They already provide literally hundreds of square feet of year-round screening. When fully grown they'll double the screening power of the berms.

I also used rosebays for screening because most of the berms are in deep shade and virtually no other shrub will bloom there. The berm along the driveway is in medium shade; it gets some late afternoon sun and quite a bit of indirect light. Here, for variety, I planted another rhododendron, 'Roseum Elegans.' My 'Roseum Elegans' are already about five feet high, and they'll grow to about eight feet—enough to hide almost all of my neighbor's house, even from my second-story windows.

For a closer look at the many other shade-tolerant shrubs, ground covers, perennials, and annuals in Evergreen, take my tour of the garden on pages 102–122.

CHOOSING FURNITURE AND SCULPTURE

Unlike other gardens, woodland gardens require almost no expensive infrastructure. In fact, the decks, steps, stairs, walls, fences, fountains, and other structures so typical of formal gardens are usually out of place in a naturalized woodland. A woodland garden needs only a few manmade accoutrements, and there are several to choose from:

- Benches or chairs on which to sit and enjoy the garden.
- Matching tables for refreshments, picnicking, and other activities.
- Birdbaths both to attract birds and to serve as focal points.
- A screened gazebo, so mosquitoes and other insects don't interfere with your enjoyment of the garden.
- Some sculpture for beauty, interest, and accent.

When choosing furnishings and sculpture, avoid the temptation to divide them into two classes. Don't think of the furnishings—the benches, chairs, tables, birdbaths, and gazebos—as utilitarian and only the sculpture as purely decorative. Every object placed in the garden, even "utilitarian" ones, must be decorative. In other words, every object (no matter how functional) must always add to, never detract from, the beauty of the site. "Useful" objects must do double duty. As John Ruskin put it, they must be both useful and beautiful. A bench, for example, must be both a comfortable place to sit and an attractive accent, a bit of sculpture in its own right. It must be just as decorative as a purely decorative object.

FURNITURE

The best woodland garden furniture, in my view, is high-quality, white-painted

A lop-eared rabbit peers over 'Emerald Gaiety' euonymus in the White Room at Evergreen.

English-style teak and white-painted Victorian-style cast iron. Both are comfortable, handsome, and durable—well-made teak will last outdoors for decades and cast iron, indefinitely. Either can serve as a year-round focal point and a strong organizing element in a garden room.

Perhaps the most valuable feature of the furniture is white paint, which provides a large bright spot of color all year round. Color (other than brown and green) is rare and hard to come by in a woodland garden. A white bench, chair, or table provides more color than a cluster of impatiens, and it does it all the time with virtually no labor other

than some fresh paint every few years. Just put the furniture in place and . . . *voila!* Automatic color.

White is usually the best color for outdoor furniture because it's brighter than almost anything else, bringing more light into the garden than almost any other color. White also provides a stronger, crisper contrast to the elements around it than virtually any other color. At the same time, it's neutral: unlike almost every other color, it doesn't run the risk of being out of place, or clashing with the garden's natural hues.

BIRDBATHS AND GAZEBOS
Because of their radial symmetry, it's easy to see birdbaths and gazebos as works of sculpture. (I think of a birdbath as a giant piece of masonry stemware and a gazebo as a large pointed monument.)

The most attractive birdbaths are graceful, with wide, over-sized bowls that lie relatively close to the ground. Birdbaths should be made of a strong and natural-looking material that harmonizes with the site, such as stone, bronze, copper, cast iron, resin compound, or concrete. Birdbaths have to be flushed out and refilled often, so install them only where you can get water to them easily.

The most attractive gazebos are usually made of wood. Like furniture, gazebos can be painted white to make strong statements.

An elegant statue and fountain are the centerpiece of Airlie's Spring Garden, which features more than an acre of pink and white azaleas.

Place them where you want a sculptural accent or where you can enjoy a good view. A screened gazebo on a hilltop is a bug-proof place to sit and watch the view below, as well as a handsome structure that both emphasizes and enhances the summit on which it rests.

SCULPTURE

Sculpture is a low-maintenance, year-round accent. In the woodland garden the best sculpture passes two tests:

- No sculpture may be truly "as lovely as a tree" but it must be beautiful enough to be worthy of being placed beside one. Like every other object added to the garden, it must add to, never subtract from, the beauty of the place.

☙ Sculpture should usually depict something one could plausibly expect to see, or at least would be pleased to see, in a woodland garden.

Unfortunately, such sculpture is rare. Most of the painted wood, plastic, and crude concrete concoctions widely available at garden centers would only make a woodland garden less attractive. You'll probably do a lot of looking before you find what you need.

Perhaps the most suitable sculptures are realistic (not cute) portrayals of woodland animals, in bronze, copper, cast iron, resin compound, or finely finished concrete. The most fitting subjects are animals that actually live in the garden or might pass through it. Realistically posed squirrels, chipmunks, rabbits, foxes, and even deer go well. Lions and giraffes, needless to say, do not. Neither do cows, horses, pigs, hens, chickens, or any other barnyard animals not usually found in the forest. Cats, dogs, or other domestic animals might be seen in the woods and, therefore, might also be appropriate.

Elaborate classical statuary is usually inappropriate, simply because it is so clearly associated with highly formal gardens. On the other hand, sculpture associated with less formal settings—a handsome Buddha, St. Francis of Assisi, or St. Fiacre, the patron saint of gardening—usually works fine. So do the lanterns and other accessories of a Japanese garden.

Whenever you choose sculpture, don't buy it just because you need some sculpture. Like any work of art, buy it because you like it—because you want to look at it so much and so often that you want to take it home with you.

Manmade objects stand out in a natural environment. That's why, in a woodland garden, a little sculpture goes a long way. Like any accent, it must be used sparingly.

A piece of sculpture is often most effective when it's the only piece in an outdoor room. Standing alone in a prominent position, with no other object competing for your attention, it may dominate and visually organize the whole space. The larger, more striking, and more prominent a sculpture, the greater its effect will be.

A sculpture can also act as a "pull-through." It can literally create motion. Positioned at the end of a path, for instance, it can pull the eye, and then the viewer, through the space and toward the sculpture for a closer look.

On the other hand, a sculpture can induce rest. Placed near a bench or seat, a lovely and intriguing human or animal figure invites one to linger and contemplate its form.

The most natural sculptures—and by far the least expensive—are stones. They too can be focal points and organizing elements.

All things equal, the most handsome and pleasing rocks are low, wide stones buried as deep as their widest dimension. A rock buried at this depth not only looks stable and restful, it also appears to be even larger than it is. You assume that the slope of the rock continues under ground and that the rock above ground is just like the tip of an iceberg: a small part of a much larger rock, or even ledge, beneath the earth. The gentler the slope of the rock above ground, the wider (and larger) you assume the entire rock to be.

If the widest point of a rock is below the ground—and it often is—dig dirt away from it until its widest part is level with the surrounding earth. The more rock you expose, the larger, wider, and generally more impressive the rock above ground will be. And the larger the rock under ground will be assumed to be (see figure 13).

On the other hand, if the widest part of the rock is above the ground, the rock will usually look top-heavy and ungainly. In that case, add enough dirt until the ground is as high as the widest part of the rock.

I brightened up Evergreen with white cast iron benches and added interest with sculpture of Buddha, the Virgin Mary, and St. Francis, as well as of frogs, rabbits, and a tortoise. To see how I placed them, take my tour of Evergreen on pages 102–122.

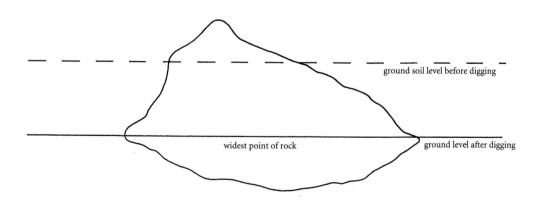

FIGURE 13: *To make a rock as impressive as possible, dig dirt away from it until its widest part is level with the ground.*

MAINTAINING THE WOODLAND GARDEN

This chapter is short for a reason: there's not much to say about maintaining a woodland garden. One of its delightful ironies is that so much garden—one with so many large plants and so much space—takes so little care.

One reason for this irony is that woodland gardens are mostly free of annual flowers and entirely free of lawns, both of which require dozens, if not hundreds, of hours of maintenance every year. Instead, woodland gardens are filled with plants that take care of themselves—trees, shrubs, and perennials that get virtually all the water they need from rain and snow and that provide their own fertilizer and their own weed-suppressing, moisture-conserving mulch from their fallen needles and leaves. Like a wild forest, a woodland garden is nature's perpetual-motion machine, a marvelous natural appliance that goes—or

grows—almost by itself. All you have to do are a few occasional chores.

One is cleaning up. Trees will continue to die or be blown over, and branches will be blown down. You'll have to clean up this debris, just as you did when you first made the garden. Much of it will accumulate over the winter, so most of it can be picked up all at once in the spring. Most, if not all, of the rest of it can be picked up on your strolls through the garden.

You may also want to rake leaves off your paths. I usually do because too many leaves can make the garden look messy and because a bare path makes a sharper contrast with, and therefore better enhances, the plants around it. (I don't rake up pine or evergreen needles because they look much neater than leaves—in fact, they make a beautiful carpet.) Often the leaves can be raked directly onto plants, adding to their mulch. The rest can be composted or hidden elsewhere in the woods. Although virtually all leaves come down in the fall, I rake them up in the spring. I prefer raking in the spring because the leaves are more compact by then, so they're less bulky and easier to handle; and, if I leave them on the ground over the winter, many will blow between the plants, so I don't have to rake them at all.

You'll also have to do at least a little weeding. Yes, the garden's shady canopy and thick natural mulch make it hard for weeds to grow, and ground covers such as pachysandra ruthlessly shade out competing plants, but some weeds will appear and you'll have to pull them up. And the sooner you do, the less the chances they'll spread. Weeds usually come up more easily in woodland gardens than in other gardens because the earth is usually more moist and looser.

The deciduous trees you cut when you first weeded the garden will send out shoots for at least several months and sometimes more than a year. To make these trees die as soon as possible, cut the shoots off as quickly and as often as you can. Remember, every leaf produced by a shoot makes food for the tree and prolongs its life. The tree will die only when it starves, and it will starve only after every leaf is gone.

The remaining trees and most shrubs in the woodland garden will rarely need pruning, but you'll have to remove an occasional

dead branch and you may choose to prune some trees and shrubs to make them fuller.

Because berms and well-chosen, well-made paths don't wear out, you'll have to do little if any grading. You may, however, have to repair erosion damage to dams and causeways and remove debris from causeway pipes.

If you have artificial pools, and you live in a cold-winter climate, you may have to drain them in the autumn. If you have goldfish, you'll probably have to put them in an indoor aquarium. You'll also have to take any frogs you can find to a real pond, where they'll be able to burrow into the mud for the winter.

Since most woodland garden plants are trees, shrubs, and perennials, virtually all the planting you'll have to do will be annuals. And you can do as much or as little of that as you wish.

If they're suited to the site, shrubs, perennials, and ground covers rarely, if ever, need watering after the first year they're planted. Most woodland plants don't need artificial fertilizer either—they get all the nutrients they need from fallen leaves, needles, and other natural waste, with qualifications:

⚬ Plants growing close to trees may lose water or nutrients to tree roots, especially during dry weather. The loss may not be life threatening, but the plants will grow fuller and faster if you give them extra water and possibly some composted cow manure or only tiny amounts of a balanced fertilizer such as granulated 10-10-10 mixture.

ꙮ Similarly, although dry periods will probably not kill woodland garden plants, watering the garden during a drought makes the plants look perkier and helps ensure optimum growth—as does a little fertilizer in the spring.

Annual flowers are another matter. They have to be watered almost every day (although not as often as annuals in less shady locations). Don't plant any more than you want to take care of and make sure they give you the biggest visual bang for your buck.

When all your maintenance chores are done, there's only one thing left to do: gather up a picnic lunch, or supper, or even breakfast, walk to one of your favorite spots in the woods, and enjoy al fresco dining in a large, lush natural garden. When that's done, consider an afternoon of reading or writing in the garden. And after you've done that. . . .

Like all woodland gardens, Evergreen took a lot of time and money to install. That, I suppose, is the bad news. The good news is that Evergreen requires little time to maintain. Each year, I rake leaves from some of the paths, remove dead branches and perhaps a dead tree, make minor repairs to the causeways, do some weeding, plant and water a few annuals, and get the fishponds ready for winter. But, mostly, Evergreen takes care of itself. In fact, it flourishes by itself.

Many summers find me traveling. When I call home and ask about the garden, my secretary doesn't tell me how this or that needs to be done—there's not much to tell. Instead she tells me how much the rhododendrons have grown, how the laurel is blooming, how the brook is running, how the vinca has spread, and how many frogs have settled in the pools. Like other woodland gardens, Evergreen often runs on automatic pilot.

PART TWO

A WOODLAND

GARDEN

TOUR

A WOODLAND GARDEN TOUR

Woodland gardens are rare. Most public and private gardens are open, sunny places dominated by vast lawns and large, often formal beds of annual and perennial flowers—the very features usually not found in woodland gardens.

And, if woodland gardens are rare, beautiful woodland gardens are rarer still. The gardens described and illustrated in this book were chosen because they're in select company: they're among the handful of landscape compositions open to the public to show us what a woodland garden should look like. Some are world famous, others less known. Some are large, some small. Many are only sections of larger gardens. Every one of them, however, is a model of the genre. All are low-maintenance, informal, naturalistic compositions that emulate the woodland in which they're found. All of them are planted in the shade of trees, most of them large. Most have extensive plantings of rhododendrons, azaleas, or other broad-leaved shrubs, most of which are evergreen and most of which produce colorful spring-time blooms. The floors of many of the gardens are planted with evergreen ground covers or perennial flowers with interesting foliage, or both.

Most importantly, all the gardens are well designed: there are enough middle- and lower-layer shrubs, ground covers, etc., so the garden feels fully planted. Most of the plants are arranged in large, irregular drifts of just one species or genus, producing simple, powerful, sometimes stunning, and always satisfying effects. All are carefully groomed, so weeds and other unwanted species don't break up the unity of the plantings. All the gardens have smooth, gently graded, gently curving, and typically unpaved paths. Every one is a learning experience.

EVERGREEN

Evergreen was designed to replicate both the privacy and extensive gardens of a large estate—but in a very unestatelike way.

Most estates create their privacy simply by setting their main house and gardens in the middle of a large tract of land—at least ten or twenty acres and usually much more. The land is so big that it automatically screens the living spaces of the estate from any development around it. That kind of privacy is expensive: it requires enough money to purchase and pay taxes on more land than most Americans ever dream of owning.

The extensive gardens of most estates are expensive, too. They usually consist of room-size beds of carefully tended flowers, hundreds of sculpted shrubs, and acres of manicured lawns—it's the most labor-intensive gardening in the world. It usually requires the services of one of more full-time gardeners—or at the very least, an owner who can spend all of his time gardening.

I can't afford even a part-time gardener, and I can't afford to garden for more than a few hours a week. So if I want a large, estatelike garden, I can't plant it with high-maintenance lawns and flower beds. I have to use low-maintenance shrubs and ground covers—plants that, once established, virtually take care of themselves and create color not just with their flowers but also with their colorful foliage.

Because my lot is less than an acre in size and surrounded by other houses, I could hardly have estatelike privacy automatically. I had to create privacy, with berms and evergreen plantings.

You've already read how Evergreen was made. To show you how it offers estatelike privacy and large, estatelike gardens, let me take you on a tour of my garden.

We'll begin at the west wing of the house, the side nearest the street. As you walk up the concrete walk toward the house, you'll notice something unusual: unlike every other house in the neighborhood—in fact, unlike almost every other house in the United States—Evergreen has no front lawn. Instead, there are thick plantings of perennial flowers, evergreen ground covers, and mainly evergreen shrubs.

Rising gently to the immediate left is a seventy-foot-long berm that begins beside the front sidewalk and runs along the street all the way to the northwest corner of the property. The lower slope at the end of the berm (which gets some afternoon sun) is planted with junipers, vinca minor, and a mugo pine (*Pinus mugo* var. *mugo*). Farther up the berm is a cluster of Japanese barberry, whose leaves are wine-red all summer long. Near the crest of the berm are rhododendrons.

Mountain laurel in front of the windows of my guest apartment helps screen unwanted views of the street. Notice how the white and green colors of the house harmonize with the white blossoms and evergreen foliage of the shrub and how the house's white facade is an excellent foil for the plants.

On the right side of the sidewalk are more junipers, vinca minor, and two low-maintenance perennials that provide color year after year: herbaceous peonies (*Paeonia* spp.) and daylilies (*Hemerocallis* spp.). Growing beside the house are large broadleaved evergreens: mountain laurel and mountain and Japanese andromeda.

Their lustrous deep green foliage is offset dramatically by the white-painted house and complemented by its dark-green shutters. Because the berm provides only partial privacy for the west wing of the house, the foundation plantings have been allowed to grow over the windows to provide year-round screening for the rooms inside. Luckily, these rooms are part of a guest apartment occupied only occasionally, and the west side of the house is not an outdoor living area. So complete privacy isn't essential here.

Before the entrance to the guest apartment, there is a dirt path off to the left, between the east slope of the berm and the large andromedas in front of the house (see photo on page 00). A quick right turn around a maple tree at the corner of the house and . . . suddenly the world around you is a very different place.

Although you're less than thirty feet from the street on the northwest side of the house and not much farther away from three other houses, they have all but disappeared thanks to the berm along the street. The berm, and the thick clusters of rhododendrons on top of it, hide almost everything outside my property. Now, instead of asphalt, cars, houses, telephone poles, and other development, you see mostly an idealized woodland: giant white pine trees, dozens of rhododendrons and other evergreen shrubs, and evergreen ground covers

spread across an amphitheater formed by the east slope of the berm on the left and by the north slope of the land ahead of you and to your right.

THE FISHPONDS

The bottom of the amphitheater, a level area close to the north side of the house, is one of the garden's few sunny places. We located two fiberglass fishponds here for several reasons:

- They can be seen and enjoyed from inside the house as well as outside, and they can be viewed every time we enter or exit the house via the back door.
- The waterlilies in the ponds need at least six hours of sunlight per day to produce their large, showy white flowers; this is one of the few places on the property where they have at least a chance of getting that much light.
- This low spot at the bottom of a hill is a natural-looking place for a pond; it's where you might find a

Opposite: This large berm and the sweep of pink-blossomed Rhododendron *'Roseum Elegans' on top of it screen the southern boundary of Evergreen.*

The bright white blossom of a waterlily and one of many frogs that enliven the ponds in Evergreen.

pond or other water features in nature.

⚘ A level place is a much easier place to install a pond than a hilly one.

You can't tell that the ponds are fiberglass because the sides are hidden by the water and the top edge is hidden by large, flat field-stones hanging over the edge. Vinca minor hides many of the spaces between the stones, helping make them look less like individual rocks and more like a continuous ledge.

Color is created by the waterlilies, drifts of red impatiens and lavender vinca blossoms, and by large goldfish, who dart about from early spring to late fall. Special interest is provided by nearly a dozen resident frogs, who come to the ponds on their own and sit like living sculpture on the gray fieldstones, waiting for mosquitoes to fly by. A graceful statue of the Virgin Mary is a strong focal point at the head of the smaller pool. Behind the other pool is a sculpture of a lop-eared rabbit standing on his hind legs and peering into the pool.

A path winds between the pools and curves gently up the north slope of the garden, between thick, lustrous evergreen carpets of pachysandra and past large white pines, rhododendrons, mountain laurel, and Japanese andromeda.

As the path nears the top of the slope, it passes a clump of variegated 'Emerald Gaiety' euonymus climbing up a small maple tree on the left. The euonymus' green-and-white evergreen foliage brightens the northwest corner of the garden year-round. The spot is made even more colorful in the summer by a cluster of variegated white-and-green hostas nearby. Both the euonymus and hostas can be glimpsed from the bottom of the path, and they provide visual incentive to walk up the path for a closer look.

On the other side of the path is an unusually striking witch hazel. The little tree rises elegantly from the earth on a single,

leaning stem and is topped by a wide, gracefully arching crown of leaves. It reminds me of one of those giant fans that servants waved over Oriental potentates to keep them cool. The tree didn't grow exactly that way—it's the product of creative pruning, which removed extraneous stems and branches and reduced the tree to this simple essence. The witch hazel is now a focal point that can be seen throughout this part of the garden.

Here the path turns to the right and runs east along the northern boundary of the property. Less than fifty feet away is my next-door neighbor's house, but you can barely see it because another berm, planted with giant rosebay rhododendrons, runs along the boundary.

Although the berm is three to four feet high, it doesn't look manmade, because it's built on the top of the amphitheater on the north side of the property. It doesn't look like an addition but a natural crest of the hill on which it's built. Also, the height and shape of the berm is irregular and divided into sections by giant glacial erratics on the crest of the hill. In fact, the erratics are so large that they provide as much screening as the berms on either side of them.

Color in this part of Evergreen is created not only by the white blossoms of the rosebay rhododendrons but also by drifts of three other evergreen shrubs: 'Emerald 'n

Gold' euonymus, which provides a bright yellow accent all year round and climbs up the large rocks in the berm; compact drooping leucothoe, whose leaves turn burgundy in winter; and Oregon grape, whose foliage becomes bronze or purple in winter. All three plants also provide a strong contrast with the rhododendrons.

Still more color is created by the large, delicate, pink, podlike blossoms of lady's-slipper orchids, which grow in a tiny, leaf-carpeted clearing next to the path. These native wildflowers appear faithfully every spring. I help them flourish by leaving them alone.

About halfway along the berm, the path comes to an intersection. To the right is a charming narrow path that winds gently back and forth down the slope of the amphitheater. As it twists past handsome granite rocks, dark green carpets of pachysandra, and more broadleaved evergreen shrubs, it provides a refreshing bird's-eye view of the large fishpond and the plantings around it.

Opposite: The Virgin Mary gazes upon a lily pool, which is surrounded by vinca and red and pink impatiens. Behind the statue is the berm, planted with rhododendrons and pachysandra, that screens Evergreen from the street.

THE NORTHEAST CORNER

Straight ahead at the intersection near the north berm is a thick bed of brown pine needles that passes between two huge white pines to enter the northeast corner of the garden.

This space is defined by a two- to three-foot-high berm, planted with rosebay rhododendrons. The junction of the northern and eastern sides of the berm helps create a charming low niche that's a perfect setting for a bright drift of yellow 'Fanfare' hosta. The hosta contrasts sharply with the rhododendrons, leucothoe, and pachysandra around it; their dark evergreen foliage makes the hosta look even brighter than it would if it grew alone. The hosta is one of Evergreen's strongest focal points and easily the most arresting element in this part of the garden.

Also in this section is 'Emerald 'n Gold' euonymus, which picks up the yellow of the hosta; large and small drifts of leucothoe; and, for accent, Japanese andromeda.

The path continues southward, past a large white pine on the right. Beside the pine is a cluster of large gray granite rocks that I made into a natural planter by filling the spaces between them with loam. The rocks hold the soil on three sides; on the fourth side the loam makes an ever-widening slope as it spills out and away from the cluster. An exuberant, room-size drift of 'Emerald Gaiety' euonymus trails over the top of the rocks, spreads around them, and is just now starting to climb the pine tree beside them.

Farther down the path, a glimpse to the left through a grove of pines and tiny witch hazels reveals the low granite cliffs on the eastern edge of the property. I removed the lower limbs of the witch hazels, which previously hid the bluffs from view. However, I left the upper limbs alone to help screen the house on top of the cliffs. This kind of trimming is an example of selective pruning, of gardening by subtraction, both to create and block a view. The cliffs are also an example of "borrowing." Because the cliffs are actually on my neighbor's land, I am borrowing them visually. In other words, I have made them a visual part of Evergreen simply by opening them up to view. Because a garden is a visual phenomenon—it includes anything you can see from the garden—borrowing is often inevitable. The object, of course, is to borrow every view you want to see by opening it up and block every view you don't with berms or other privacy barriers.

Almost immediately after you see the cliffs, you'll come to a pair of large rocks, opposite one another, that are just high enough to be natural benches. While seated here, you can enjoy close, eye-level views of large plantings all around you—rhododendrons, Japanese andromedas, leucothoe, and 'Emerald Gaiety' euonymus.

THE PATIO

The patio is located on the east side of the house. This irregularly shaped natural courtyard, paved with large, flat, unevenly cut gray slate stones, is a snug place. It's ringed by large, handsome granite boulders, large trees, and a low berm planted with rosebay rhododendrons, vinca minor, 'Emerald 'n Gold' euonymus, and white-and-green variegated hostas. The rocks, trees, berm, and rosebays create a comforting sense of enclosure and hide neighboring houses to the east of the property. When you're sitting in the screened porch on the west side of the patio, a woodland garden surrounds you on three sides.

To add even more color to the patio, I placed six classical urns around the perimeter and planted them with pink impatiens. The urns are made of gray concrete; like the gray paving stones, they harmonize well with the gray granite rocks in the surrounding woodland. In the middle of the patio, I placed white Victorian-style cast-iron furniture: a bench and two chairs around a small table. They're valued as much, if not more, for their bright, year-round, low-maintenance color as they are for their utility.

On the west side of the patio, in a corner created by the porch and the house, is a small, slightly raised area thickly planted with rhododendrons, leucothoe, and pachysandra. The focal point of the planting is a handsome concrete sculpture of

Buddha, sitting among the plants in the lotus position. By his presence, he makes this peaceful spot even more serene.

Another sculpture, a tortoise, decorates the flat top of a large rock on the south side of the patio.

The north side of the patio is the end of a wide, steep slope that springs up from one side of the house. This hillside is one of the garden's rare semisunny spots, so I planted it with hydrangeas. These fast-growing, deciduous bushes tolerate light shade and produce large blue flowers that last for weeks in mid-summer and provide color for months after they fade. The slope where they're planted was gouged out of the woods when the house was built. It was all but bare of topsoil. Before I planted the hydrangeas—which need rich, moist soil—I dug large holes, dumped the excavated dirt into berms, and refilled the holes with loam enriched with peat moss and composted manure. On top of the slope, the long woody stems of rockspray cotoneasters (*Cotoneaster* spp.) arch gracefully over gray granite rocks; in the fall these low, sprawling shrubs are festooned with red berries.

At the foot of the slope is a highbush blueberry (*Vaccinium corymbosum*), whose berries attract lots of birds. Hanging from the bush is a hummingbird feeder, which attracts many darting hummingbirds. A few feet away is a concrete birdbath that's a focal point for the north side of the patio as well

The gray slate paving and gray concrete urns harmonize with the gray granite rocks at the edge of the patio at Evergreen. Spring color is provided by the rhododendron and vinca flowers, seasonal color by the red impatiens and variegated hosta, and year-round color by the variegated evergreen 'Emerald 'n Gold' euonymus and the evergreen foliage of the rhododendrons and vinca.

as a source of frequent entertainment as robins, blue jays, and other birds vigorously churn the water. We have a close view of the birds from a screened porch, which serves as our dining room from mid-spring to mid-fall.

THE MIRADOR

From the patio you re-enter the woods and follow a path that gently descends past large rocks, evergreen shrubs, and carpets of pachysandra. Just past a large drift of 'Emerald 'n Gold' euonymus on the left and a large cluster of rhododendrons on the right, the easy descent is interrupted by a low berm that curves gracefully across the path. The level, terraced space just in front of the berm provides one of Evergreen's grandest views: the entire southeast corner of the garden. I named this spot the Mirador, after the lovely Spanish word for viewpoint.

Directly below the Mirador is the steep slope leading down to the brook. You have a bird's-eye view of the rhododendrons, mountain laurels, vinca, pachysandra, and patches of ferns on the brook's relatively sunny West Bank and the barberry bushes and jewelweed on the shadier East Bank. Farther up the East Bank are more striking granite cliffs.

This viewpoint used to be nothing more than the upper part of the steep slope that the Mirador now overlooks, but a few dozen wheelbarrow loads of fill transformed the site into a graceful woodland balcony. I planted leucothoe on it because it's low growing; it decorates the balcony nicely but

Buddha meditates in a bed of pachysandra and rhododendrons.

A large drift of white variegated hosta provides season-long color in the south-central part of Evergreen. Notice the pine tree at left, the pachysandra at the lower left, the ferns at the lower right and right rear, and the leucothoe amid the hosta, which contributes variety and year-round foliage.

it doesn't hide the view. I chose 'Girard's Rainbow' leucothoe because its new foliage is a lively mixture of yellow, green, and pinkish-red—an exciting plant for an exciting spot.

A path follows the curve of the Mirador, then runs beside a large, handsome rock at the end of the viewpoint and descends to one of Evergreen's most striking features: an enormous, sixteen-by-twenty-two-foot drift of white-and-green variegated hosta planted on a steep, rock-studded slope. The hosta cluster is large enough and bright enough to make an impact from more than fifty feet away. Set off by the green foliage all around it and raised by its sloping bed, it's an enormous creamy focal point that can be seen throughout the entire south-central part of the garden.

THE WHITE ROOM

The path makes a loop around the hosta, offering you close views of its unusually colorful leaves. Then the trail turns right and passes between a large rock and a steep, rhododendron-planted berm. This brings you to the White Room.

If you sit on the white cast-iron bench by the entrance, you'll see how this space

Evergreen's White Room is named after the white colors of the cast-iron bench, the variegated hosta and euonymus, the impatiens (top of rock, left) and the blossoms of the rosebay rhododendrons (upper left, rear).

earned its name. Along the east side of the room, which is roughly fifteen feet wide and twenty feet long, is a low berm, an extension of the higher one just outside the room. The tops of both berms are planted with rosebay rhododendrons. The berm and the rhododendrons form the east wall of the room and screen it from the houses to the east. The west side of the room is a tight cluster of boulders. Among the rocks are large white pines and more rosebays. Together, the rocks, pines, and rhododendrons form the west wall of the room. The south wall, directly opposite the bench, is the flat face of the biggest boulder in the garden. This gigantic rock is fifteen feet wide at its base tapering up to a twelve-foot-high peak near its center. A rhododendron and a Japanese andromeda are planted at the base of the rock to emphasize its dramatic configuration. Beneath the rock and all around the edges of the White Room are drifts of 'Emerald Gaiety' euonymus. In front of the euonymus at the base of the large rock is a cluster of white variegated hosta. In the center of the euonymus on the west wall of the room is a small cluster of white impatiens.

Both the plantings and the white bench create a dramatic concentric gradation of color: in the outermost ring, at the edge of the room, are the dark green leaves and white blossoms of the rhododendrons; just inside that is the white-and-light-green

White impatiens surrounded by 'Emerald Gaiety' euonymus in the White Room.

foliage of the euonymus; and within the euonymus are the white-and-green hostas, the bright white blooms of the impatiens, and the pure white bench. The bench, in fact, provides so much color that it's a focal point for anyone in the White Room who isn't sitting on it. For added interest, and a bit of contrast, there's a fine, realistic, lifesize gray sculpture of a rabbit standing on his hind legs and peeking out from the euonymus below the large rock.

You can leave the White Room alongside an unusual large, low rock whose flat top and straight sides meet, tablelike, at a right

A large drift of graceful hay-scented ferns grows around a white pine.

angle. Then a curving path cuts through the room-size patch of hay-scented ferns just beside the rock and below a large drift of green-and-white euonymus. A stroll through the three-foot-high ferns leads farther down the slope of the garden as the path curves to the west, affording you a long, wide view back up the slope. In the foreground are the lush, light green fronds of the ferns. Above the ferns is the creamy, green-tinted drift of hosta. Beyond the hostas and stretching away into the distance on all sides are masses of evergreen foliage—pachysandra, rhododendrons, andromeda—that are the essence of the

garden. To the right of the ferns are the rocks and rhododendrons at the edge of the White Room. In front of the ferns is another statue of Buddha. This low statue does more than add interest to the scene; it also expands it by drawing your eyes down and to the left, making everything behind it and to the right look larger, higher, and more massive.

THE GOLD ROOM

As the path heads to the east, it passes close to one of the largest white pines in the garden. The trail curves around a low berm planted with rhododendrons and passes a cluster of andromedas and a large, three-foot-high, flat-topped rock with Canadian mayflowers growing thickly all over the top of it. Like the other Canadian mayflowers on the property, they grew there with absolutely no assistance from me. They're another generous gift of nature.

Past the Canadian mayflower-bedecked rock is the entrance to the Gold Room, named for the 'Emerald 'n Gold' euonymus that grows all around its edge and the

Opposite: Year-round color in the Gold Room is provided by the white bench, the 'Emerald 'n Gold' euonymus growing up the sheer boulder on either side of the bench, and the vinca in the lower left. The path is covered with pine needles.

yellow-leafed coleus that flourish in the center of the thirty-by-forty-foot space. The Gold Room is one of my favorite places in the garden, and the view from the large white cast-iron bench on the south side of the room reveals why.

Opposite the bench is the face of the huge boulder that forms the south wall of the White Room. The south face of this boulder is even more striking than the north face. It's flat, sheer, almost vertical, and even wider and taller than the north face. Just like the north face, however, it tapers like a Gothic window up to a center peak. On the ground below the peak, at the center of the rock, I placed a small, white cast-iron bench. The white bench not only sets off the gray rock, it also brings your eye down to the bottom of the boulder, both emphasizing and visually increasing its impressive height.

The east wall of the Gold Room is a large, gently sloping, thirty-foot-long berm that's about six feet high at each end and rises to about ten feet high in the center. The berm and rosebay rhododendrons on top of it

Yellow coleus provides summer-long color in the Gold Room. A solid drift of vinca grows beneath the planter, and rosebay rhododendrons are at the rear on the berm at the edge of the room.

screen out houses to the east. The south wall of the room is formed by a rosebay rhododendron behind the bench on this side of the room and the flat wall of another big boulder—about eight feet tall and fourteen feet long—just beside the bench. The west wall is a cluster of pine trees, rocks, and evergreen shrubs.

Creeping up the giant rocks and trees around the edge of the room are three dozen 'Emerald 'n Gold' euonymus. High above the floor of the room is a soaring canopy of branches reaching out from the encircling pines.

In the center of the room is a large patch of vinca, about eight feet across. On the eastern edge of the vinca are a few large rocks that I enhanced by digging the dirt away from their outer edges (the edges farthest away from the vinca). This excavation not only made the stones look larger, it also made the vinca patch more interesting and more impressive because it raised one edge of the clump more than a foot above the path beside it.

In the center of the vinca is a graceful, low, concrete planter thickly planted with yellow-leafed coleus. Placing just a few bright flowers near the optical center of a space was a favorite trick of Moorish gardeners. Properly placed, just a few such plants can dominate a space and make the entire room look well planted. The viewer is too busy looking at the flowers to notice

that there are really not many of them. Thanks in part to this small but carefully chosen and positioned planting, the Gold Room has bright, summer-long color that requires little maintenance. (The coleus needs only occasional watering because the Gold Room is shady, the leaves of the plants provide even more shade, and the planting soil is nearly one-half peat moss to retain a lot of water.)

The concrete planter, incidentally, is actually a large, graceful birdbath sunk deep into the ground, so only the thick part of its pedestal is visible. Its already wide bowl looks even wider—and more impressive—closer to the ground and the pedestal looks more impressive with some of its frivolous details buried. I drilled three holes in the bottom of the bowl for drainage, using a carbide bit designed for drilling concrete. I used this birdbath as a planter for four reasons:

- Its wide bowl holds a larger, more impressive cluster of flowers than a narrow trough.
- The wide bowl looks lower than it actually is, and the lower it looks, the higher the giant rock on the north wall of the garden looks by comparison.
- The birdbath cost less than real planters with much less attractive and less useful shapes.

✆ It's made of gray concrete, which unifies the space because both its color and texture echo the garden's gray granite rocks.

The large bench in the Gold Room is a soothing spot for picnicking, reading, and daydreaming. When seated there, the man-made world seems absent; instead you're surrounded, almost embraced, by giant rocks, immense pines, and large evergreen shrubs.

THE BROOK

In the northeast corner of the Gold Room, at the northern end of the berm, is a small passageway between two large rocks. This rock gate leads right to the West Bank of the brook that is visible from the Mirador.

The lower West Bank is one of the largest clearings, and, therefore, one of the sunnier spots in the garden. It's one of just a few places in Evergreen where mountain laurels and rhododendrons (other than rosebays) will bloom profusely. I planted the slope with both laurels and thick drifts of 'Roseum Elegans' rhododendrons. On the hill to the left of the path I also exposed an impressive steplike formation of several small boulders simply by digging dirt away from them—another example of gardening by subtraction (or perhaps I should say grading by subtraction).

On the edge of the slope of the West Bank, just outside the stone gate to the Gold Room, the path forks.

The left fork leads down the slope and passes through a group of large mossy rocks close to the brook. The rocks are now both unified and softened by pachysandra planted between them. From there the path winds upstream or to the right. The path to

The brook splatters on moss-covered rocks at the edge of the large pool formed by the lower causeway.

Solid drifts of jewelweed at the base of the cliffs on the East Bank of the brook.

the right leads past some honeysuckles and quickly comes to a dramatic viewpoint overlooking the large pool formed by the lower of two causeways.

Going right at the fork on the other side of the stone gate leads down the slope to the south of the rock-and-pachysandra garden to the lower causeway. The causeway crosses over to the East Bank, providing a view of the pool and the cascades upstream, and the path passes barberries and jewelweed as it travels upstream along the east side of the brook.

The upper causeway crosses back over to the West Bank and the path leads upstream past large drifts of ferns on the left and sheer cliffs on the other side of the brook.

The path ends where the brook flows over the top of a wide, flat rock in a mesmerizing wide, thin fall. Here you also have a long view upstream that includes a picturesque log that has fallen across the brook.

Another path travels back downstream where, upon reaching the lower West Bank, it curves around charming maple trees with beautiful gnarled trunks.

THE CAVE

From the brook the path takes you back through the Gold Room and west to a tall, narrow opening of a the Cave in the distance. Like many small "caves," this one isn't a true cavern but simply one enormous boulder leaning against another. But it's still an interesting garden feature—about two feet wide, six feet high, and ten feet deep—so I built a side path to it and planted 'Emerald 'n Gold' euonymus beneath it to call attention to it.

Maple leaves above the Cave are backlit by late afternoon sun.

A trip back up the main path winds through an allée of 'Emerald Gaiety' euonymus as it climbs up to the driveway.

Although Evergreen is a private residential garden, anyone who wants to see it can do so without charge. The garden is open to the public every year—usually for a consecutive Friday, Saturday, and Sunday in either early June when the 'Roseum Elegans' rhododendrons are in bloom, or in mid-July when the rosebay rhododendrons are flowering. The garden can also be seen by appointment. Feel free to call me at 603-497-8020 for more information.

THE ASTICOU TERRACES

Like all natural-looking gardens, a woodland garden isn't imposed on a site like paint on a blank canvas—like the vast, flat, formal French gardens of La Notre, for example. Instead, it reflects, indeed expresses, the special character of the site, what Alexander Pope called "the Genius of the Place."

Opposite: It's difficult to tell what parts of the Asticou Terraces were built by Joseph Henry Curtis and what parts were made by nature. The lowbush blueberries and sheep laurel (at right) and dark green spruces all grow wild on Mount Desert Island, and the stones blend flawlessly with the surrounding cliffs.

The natural and manmade elements of the Asticou Terraces are deftly blended. Its paving, steps, and walls are made of the same gray granite as its cliffs.

The genius of the Maine coast is dark, brooding evergreens looming over rough, gray granite rocks and cliffs. The landscape architect Joseph Henry Curtis consulted this genius well when he created the Asticou Terraces at his summer home on Mount Desert Island, Maine.

Curtis built the Terraces on the spruce-covered cliffs that spring up steeply from the shores of Northeast Harbor. You explore the Terraces on a smooth gravel path that makes a series of long gentle switchbacks up the granite bluffs. You barely start walking up the path before you realize that the Terraces are a simple place. Like much of the Maine coast they're mostly spruces and granite. The few other trees—mostly pines and white cedars—are not even noticed at first because they're almost all evergreens and they blend in so well with the spruces. Granite, too, is everywhere—in the cliffs, the boulders, and the low stone walls that line the trail; in the occasional short flights of rock steps in the path; in the stone pavings of the upper path; and even in the stone walls of the handsome shelter where you can sit on rustic wooden benches and enjoy the view of Northeast Harbor. Beneath the deep shade of the evergreens much of the ground is covered only with an endless, solid carpet of brown spruce nee-dles. The only other plants are the mosses and lichens on the rocks, a few ferns, and patches of lowbush blueberries (*Vaccinium angustifolium*) and sheep laurel—all plants that, on Mount Desert Island, are as common as grass in Ireland.

In fact, so faithful to the site was Curtis' design that you can't tell how much of the Terraces was made by him and how much was made by nature. It appears as if nature did most of the work.

Paradoxically, however, this minimalism is Curtis' most valuable contribution to his creation. His apparent willingness to let nature do most of the work makes the Terraces easy to maintain and, more importantly, his restraint—his repetition mainly of just two materials, spruces and granite—gives the Terraces an awesome simplicity.

The Asticou Terraces are now owned by the nonprofit Asticou Terraces Trust, which also administers the Thuya Lodge (Curtis' former summer residence) and the adjacent Thuya Garden (a formal flower garden) at the top of the Terraces.

The Terraces are open year-round. The Lodge is open July 1 to Labor Day from 10:00 A.M. to 4:30 P.M. The Thuya Garden is open July through September from dawn to dusk. There's a two-dollar admission fee to enter the garden.

The entrance to the Terraces is on Route 3, in the Asticou section of Northeast Harbor, less than half a mile south of the intersection of Route 3 and Route 198. The parking area is on the west (ocean) side of Route 3; the Terraces are on the other side.

For more information, call 207-276-5130, or write the Asticou Terraces Trust, P.O. Box 1120, Northeast Harbor, ME 04662-1120.

PINE HILL, CENTRAL PARK

Contrary to what many people think, Central Park isn't New York City's version of a national park—a reservation created to protect a beautiful, unspoiled natural area from development. Central Park's lovely meadows, lakes, and natural-looking, gently rolling, tree-shaded terrain were not made by nature. They were made by Frederick Law Olmsted—considered to be America's first landscape architect—and his partner, the architect Calvert Vaux. When Olmsted and Vaux started building Central Park in the 1850s, the site was a nearly treeless, partly swampy wasteland dotted with, among other things, pigsties, squatters' shacks, and other eyesores. To give the land a more interesting shape, Olmsted and Vaux made some of the low spots lower and filled many of them with lakes and ponds, and they made some of the high spots higher by building them up with dirt.

One of the park's most charming high spots is Pine Hill, a wooded knoll near the southwest shore of the Lake. Pine Hill is barely thirty feet high and two hundred feet across, but it's a notable example of fine woodland planting and path-making.

To find it, walk along the path beside the Lake, between the Loeb Boathouse on the eastern end of the Lake and the grand Bethesda Terrace and Fountain to the southwest. About halfway between the boathouse and the terrace, look to the south (away from the Lake), and you'll see a knoll densely planted with broadleaved evergreen shrubs. That's Pine Hill.

The walkway up Pine Hill first passes between small clusters of boulders, then

A squirrel on the rustic Adirondack bench on the summit of Pine Hill in Central Park. The evergreen foliage of the Japanese andromeda and pine trees behind the bench provide year-round interest.

The rosebay rhododendrons on Pine Hill after a rain shower. The large, bright white blossoms appear in late June.

curves clockwise, to the right, and keeps curving to the right, all the way to the top of the knoll. The curve does several things: because it makes the climb gradual, it also makes it gentle, almost effortless. And because the curve makes the walk longer, it also makes Pine Hill seem larger than it really is. Most importantly, the curve creates progressive realization: the plantings near the top of the knoll are hidden at first behind the broad bend in the path; they're gradually revealed only as you walk up the hill. Finally, the path bends even more sharply to the right and reveals the two biggest surprises of the walk: the flat crest of the knoll, which you don't see until you are

English ivy and rosebay rhododendrons are among the lush evergreen plantings on Pine Hill.

actually on it, and an eleven-foot-wide rustic Adirondack-style bench. The oversized bench is a pleasant place to sit but its greatest importance is visual: it's an impressive and appropriate bit of sculpture that not only defines the summit of Pine Hill and the thick evergreen plantings around it but also characterizes Pine Hill as a tiny bit of upstate wilderness in the middle of Manhattan. The bench, the flatness of the summit, and the end of the long rightward curve in the walkway are all invitations to pause and enjoy the views. From this shady and secluded aerie you can catch glimpses, through the trees, of both the lake and the

immense bowl-shaped fountain on Bethesda Terrace.

Shade is provided mainly by Austrian black pines (*Pinus nigra*), plus a few white pines and some Canadian hemlocks, river birches (*Betula nigra*), gray birches (*B. populifolia*), and black cherries (*Prunus serotina*). Most of the evergreen shrubs are rosebay rhododendrons, which in New York City usually bloom in late June. Other evergreen shrubs, which provide welcome variety and interest, are Manhattan euonymus on the left (east) side of the path; leucothoe, notably near the bottom of the path; and Japanese andromeda, mostly near the top of the hill. All are arranged in attractive clusters. On the ground are wide drifts of English ivy and purpleleaf wintercreeper. These tough, vigorous ground covers withstand abuse and suppress weeds—especially welcome characteristics in busy Central Park, where plants are subject to all sorts of degradation and there aren't enough groundskeepers to pull up every weedy invader.

Pine Hill's all-evergreen palette provides not only a year-round array of stunning evergreen foliage but also a tiny, quiet woodland retreat in the middle of New York City.

Like all New York City parks, Central Park is open every day of the year. There is no admission fee. The park entrance closest to Pine Hill is at Fifth Avenue and East 72nd

Street; there's a map of the park near the entrance. A printed map of the park is available at the Central Park Visitor Center, in the historic Dairy. The park has several good restaurants—including one at the Boathouse—as well as many foodcarts selling hot dogs and other snacks.

PEIRCE'S WOODS, LONGWOOD GARDENS

Located in the historic Brandywine Valley in southeastern Pennsylvania, Longwood is renowned for its large formal gardens, the elaborate plant displays in its immense conservatories, and the unparalleled water displays created by its hundreds of fountains. Soon, however, Longwood will also be known for one of the most original and beautiful woodland gardens in America.

The new garden is in Peirce's Woods, a five-acre woodland sloping gently down to the lake at the eastern end of the site. Peirce's Woods is named after the family that once owned the land and planted many of its giant trees. Until recently, the woods were planted with lots of Asian hybrid rhododendrons and other exotic flora. But as a sign at the edge of the woods explains, the renovation of Peirce's Woods is designed to make the garden "more in keeping with the Peirce heritage of collecting and using native plants." Most of the exotics have been or will be removed and, as the sign goes on to explain, "ornamental selections of native

woodland trees, shrubs, and herbaceous plants are being used in masses among the spectacular overstory trees to create a work of art inspired by the Eastern North American deciduous forest."

Too often, native plants mean dull plants. Thanks to landscape architect W. Gary Smith's splendid design, however, the new plants in Peirce's Woods will be anything but boring. Under the high canopy of sugar maples (*Acer saccharum*), oaks, and tulip trees (*Liriodendron tulipifera*), huge, ragged drifts of foam flower make long sweeps from one side of the path to the other and deep into the woods—sometimes so deep they almost disappear from view. In the spring the effect is stunning: the forest is covered with vast undulating carpets of bright white flower stalks. In the fall, the foliage turns bronze-purple. Complementing the foam flower are large irregular drifts of heuchera—*H. villosa*, *H. americana* 'Dale's Strain,' and the purple *H. americana* 'Garnet.' The interesting foliage of these plants adds rich texture to the forest floor from early spring to late fall. For variety, there are also sweeps of Allegheny pachysandra (*P. procumbens*), which has slightly mottled leaves, Christmas ferns (*Polystichum acrostichoides*), trilliums, mayapple (*Podophyllum peltatum*), creeping phlox (*Phlox stolonifera*), golden star (*Chrysogonum virginianum*), and wild columbine (*Aquilegia canadensis*), whose

Seemingly endless sweeps of foam flower create a stunning cream-and-dark-green spring carpet in Peirce's Woods. (Photo by Larry Albee of Longwood Gardens.)

intricate blossoms poised, on delicate, almost invisible stalks seem to hover magically in midair.

There are also patches of drooping leucothoe (*L. fontanesiana*), native azaleas (*R. austrinum*), mountain andromeda (*Pieris floribunda*), American holly (*Ilex opaca*), and oakleaf hydrangeas (*H. quercifolia*). Unlike most woodland gardens, however, shrubs play only a minor role in this one, both because they're used sparingly, as accents, and because, unlike the colorful exotic rhododendrons they replaced, their blossoms are subtle and muted. In this garden, for a change, the stars are herbaceous ground covers.

Peirce's Woods isn't quite as colorful as gardens filled with exotic rhododendrons and other bright-flowered shrubs, and it doesn't have the year-round impact of an evergreen garden. Thanks especially to Smith's dramatic design—interesting and often beautiful perennials arranged in vast naturalistic drifts—the revised Peirce's Woods shows that native wildflowers can be made into an idealized woodland garden that's an exhilarating work of landscape art.

Longwood is open every day of the year, 9:00 A.M. to 6:00 P.M. from April through October, and 9:00 A.M. to 5:00 P.M. from November through March. The Conservatories always open at 10:00 A.M. Admission is ten dollars for adults (six dollars on Tuesdays), six dollars for people ages sixteen to twenty; and two dollars for children ages six to fifteen. Children under six are admitted free.

Longwood's fine Terrace Restaurant offers outdoor dining with a view of the gardens, and its Garden Shop has a large selection of books.

Longwood is located on Route 1, about three miles northeast of Kennett Square, Pennsylvania, thirty miles west of Philadelphia, and twelve miles north of Wilmington, Delaware. To reach the garden, take Route 1 and watch for the signs for Longwood.

For more information, call 610-388-1000, or write Longwood Gardens, P.O. Box 501, Kennett Square, PA 19348-0501.

WINTERTHUR GARDEN

Located just six miles from each other, both Longwood and Winterthur were the life's work of men who believed in building beauty in the grand manner—and who had a family fortune to do it with. But while Pierre S. du Pont's Longwood Gardens are a monument to formality, Henry Francis du Pont's Winterthur is a masterpiece of naturalism.

You begin to experience Winterthur's woodland gardens immediately after you park your car and start walking down the paved path toward the Visitor Pavilion. Like many of the paths at Winterthur, this one curves through a mature deciduous woodland of large old oaks, maples, tulip trees, and dogwoods. First, you pass drifts of drooping leucothoe and sweet box. As you get closer to the Pavilion, the plantings get larger, thicker, and more impressive: Japanese andromeda and drifts of pachysandra, violets, and mayapples; mountain laurel; rhododendrons; and, finally, solid carpets of pachysandra covering the ground in front of the Pavilion.

After passing through the Pavilion, you re-enter the woods on the paved Pavilion

Pink and white kurume azaleas blanket Winterthur's Azalea Woods. (Photo by Linda Eirhart of Winterthur.)

grant lavender flowers of *R.* 'Winterthur' add contrast and variety.

At the very top of the hill is a small white wooden structure, about the size of a small arbor, with a low, green hoodlike roof. The structure is actually a charming elliptical gate that you'll pass through shortly. From this vantage point, however, it serves another purpose: with its pointed top, it makes a perfect finial for the top of the hill. Plus, it's a focal point, drawing your attention up from the path to all the azaleas on the hillside. It makes you want to climb the hill for a closer look at the intriguing and mysterious bit of sculpture.

Almost immediately you'll make a sharp left and follow an unpaved path upward, through what you now see is a gate. Winterthur's unpaved paths, incidentally, are an inspiration: they look like plain dirt trails, but they're actually made of red gravel quarried in the area, so they're durable as well as natural looking.

The path curves past rhododendrons, mayapples, and other wildflowers, crosses under the road again, and takes you into one of the greatest woodland gardens ever made—the Azalea Woods.

Walk, passing under a handsome stone bridge on which tour buses drive over the walkway. On the right side of the walk, large, solid drifts of soft green ferns contrast splendidly with the hard gray stones of the bridge. On the left, the high, steep bank is covered with large, natural-looking drifts of azaleas underplanted with violets. In early May the slope is covered with the white blossoms of *Rhododendron mucronatum* cv. 'Magnifica.' Farther up the hillside, the fra-

Opposite: Red, white, and stunning fuchsia azaleas in the Azalea Woods. The white blossoms are echoed by the white bracts of the dogwoods. (Photo by Linda Eirhart of Winterthur.)

The Azalea Woods are eight acres of open woodlands whose middle layer consists of almost nothing but kurume azaleas (*Rhododendron* var. *kurume*). In early May, you walk through seemingly endless allées of colors: vast, harmonious drifts of whites, pinks, lavender, with a little red and a touch of orange for a little spice (or, as Harry du Pont put it, "to chic it up"). Still more color is provided by dogwoods, which bloom when the azaleas do, and by Dexter rhododendrons near the edge of the woods. On the forest floor du Pont planted trilliums, Solomon's-seal, violets, phlox, columbine, mayapple, lots of Spanish bluebells, and other shade-loving perennials. When the azaleas are in bloom, however, your eyes are rarely on the floor of this dazzling outdoor room.

The Winterthur garden is open Monday through Saturday from 9:00 A.M. to dusk, and Sunday from noon to 5:00 P.M. (except for Thanksgiving, Christmas, and New Year's Day). Admission is eight dollars for adults, six dollars for seniors and students, and four dollars for children ages five through eleven. Children under five are admitted free.

The Visitor Pavilion serves breakfast, lunch, afternoon tea, and Sunday brunch.

Opposite: A harmonious tapestry of pink, white, and lavender blossoms carpets the eight acres of woods. (Photo by Linda Eirhart of Winterthur.)

The Pavilion store has a large selection of gardening books.

Winterthur is located on Route 52 in Delaware, six miles northwest of Wilmington, five miles south of Route 1 (in Pennsylvania) and six miles south of Longwood Gardens. If you're approaching Winterthur from the south on Interstate 95, take exit 7; if you're approaching the garden from the north on Interstate 95, take exit 7B; in either case, follow Delaware Avenue and take the left fork onto Pennsylvania Avenue (Route 52).

For more information, call 1-800-448-3883 or 302-888-4600, TTY 302-888-4907, or write Winterthur, Winterthur, DE 19735.

AIRLIE GARDENS
This too-little-known pleasure ground in Wilmington, North Carolina, is one of the most satisfying woodland gardens in America. It's charm comes from its lush but simple plantings and its easy, unforced naturalism.

You start liking Airlie the minute you drive through its gates. You follow narrow dirt roads that wind gracefully through a mature, open forest of live oaks (*Quercus virginiana*), pines, magnolias, and dogwoods. Lining the roads are seemingly endless solid drifts of ivy, vinca, and fuchsia-colored azaleas.

Lawns are the exception, not the rule, at Airlie, and annual and perennial flowers are

Vast sweeps of white and pink azaleas carpet the Spring Garden at Airlie.

species that allow the entire 155-acre garden to be maintained by only four people.

One of the most beautiful parts of Airlie is the Spring Garden. Its focal point is a lovely, copper-colored classical statue of a woman balancing a jug of water on her right shoulder and holding another jug in her left hand by her side. Water drips from both jugs, soaking almost the entire statue in a glistening wet glaze; it then trickles into the twelve-foot-wide circular bowl the woman is standing in. The gentle dripping and splashing both looks and sounds cool, especially on a warm day.

The statue rests amid more than an acre of azaleas, a solid planting that runs as much as two hundred feet in every direc- tion, broken only by the grassy paths wind- ing between them. In April, the shrubs make a vast, harmonious tapestry of colors—great splotches of white, pink, and lavender—that stretches into the surrounding woods. So far does the color extend that, from the statue, the azaleas look not like shrubs but like a tall, billowing ground cover.

Almost as stunning as the Spring Garden are the solid drifts of fuchsia azaleas that carpet the wooded banks of the long lake in the center of the garden. The colors are reflected in, and offset by, the dark waters of the lake. Adding motion, interest, and color at the same time, graceful white swans and Canada geese glide across the water.

even more rare. The plantings are mainly trees, azaleas, camellias, and evergreen ground covers—relatively low-maintenance

If the poet Wordsworth had rambled about Airlie instead of the English Lake District, he might have written not about a crowd of golden daffodils but about hosts of azaleas:

Beside the lake, beneath the trees . . .
Continuous as the stars that shine
And twinkle on the Milky Way,
They stretched in never-ending line
Along the margin of a bay.

White and pink azaleas create a strong contrast with the dark green ivy growing up the sprawling limbs of a live oak at the edge of the Spring Garden.

Massive beds of pink azaleas line the wooded shores of the lake at Airlie; white dogwoods bloom above.

Like many Low Country gardens, Airlie was once a rice plantation. Today it's owned by the descendants of W. Albert Corbett, a planter and manufacturer in Wilmington.

Airlie is open from 8:00 A.M. to 6:00 P.M. from March 1 through April 30, and 9:00 A.M. to 5:00 P.M. from May 1 to the first weekend in October. Admission is six dollars for adults and five dollars for seniors from March 1 through April 30, five dollars for adults and four dollars for seniors the rest of the season. Children under thirteen are admitted free.

The gardens are on Airlie Road in Wilmington. To get there, take Route 17 to Route 74, then turn right onto the Military

Cutoff Road and left onto Airlie Road at the four-way intersection of the Military Cutoff Road, Route 76, Wrightsville Avenue, and Airlie Road.

For more information, call 1-800-334-0684 or 910-763-4646, or write Airlie Gardens, P.O. Box 210, Wilmington, NC 28402-0210.

MIDDLETON PLACE

Located just up the Ashley River from Charleston, South Carolina, Middleton Place is justly renowned as one of America's largest and most beautiful formal gardens. But Middleton also has a woodland-and-water garden that, especially in springtime, rivals Airlie's.

Pink azaleas blooming in the woods around Cypress Lake at Middleton Place.

The garden surrounds Cypress Lake, a small pond in the woods on the northern perimeter of the formal gardens. In the eighteenth century, the pond was one of several on the plantation used to irrigate rice fields along the Ashley River. Today, however, the placid, shady pond is the centerpiece of a sumptuously beautiful composition. Under the shade of live oaks and other hardwoods and bald cypress trees (*Taxodium distichum*), solid sweeps of indica azaleas (*Rhododendron* var. *indica*) grow all around the edge of the little lake. In the spring, the scene is dazzling. Three- to four-inch-wide, trumpet-shaped flowers nearly cover the bushes, and the banks of the pond are carpeted with an endless swath of color: huge drifts of blazing pink and fuchsia blossoms with splotches of white for contrast, all multiplied by their reflections in the dark, mirror-smooth water of the pond. The wide, smooth, soft gravel path that circles the lake takes you beside soft, chest-high walls of azalea blossoms, giving you close, continuous views of color.

Middleton Place is open from 9:00 A.M. to 5:00 P.M. every day of the year. Admission to the gardens is twelve dollars for adults;

Opposite: Fuchsia azaleas seen through bald cypress trees on Cypress Lake. Notice the irises in the foreground and the reflections of the azaleas in the smooth, dark water.

eleven dollars for seniors, students, AAA members, and members of the armed services; and six dollars for children ages six through twelve. Children under six are admitted free.

Middleton is on Ashley River Road (Route 61), about fourteen miles northwest of Charleston. To reach Middleton from Interstate 26, turn onto Interstate 526 and then north onto Ashley River Road. From Highway 17 South, turn onto Bees Ferry Road, then north onto Ashley River Road. From Route 17 North, turn directly onto Ashley River Road.

For more information, call 803-556-6020, or write Middleton Place, Ashley River Road, Charleston, SC 29414-7206.

CALLAWAY GARDENS

Callaway Gardens, in Pine Mountain, Georgia, is part of a large, spiffy twenty-five-hundred-acre resort and convention center that includes twelve stores, eight restaurants, four golf courses, dozens of cottages and villas, and a three-hundred-fifty-room hotel. Happily, none of these facilities detract from the beauty of the site because they're scattered unobtrusively among the pleasant open pine woods typical of the west Georgia uplands.

Many of Callaway's gardens consist of trails winding among large collections of shrubs and wildflowers scattered through the woods. Callaway's most beautiful

Pink rhododendrons under oaks and loblolly pines along the Azalea Trails.

woodland gardens, however, are the Azalea Trails near little Mockingbird Lake, one of thirteen manmade but natural-looking ponds on the grounds.

The trails are wide, smooth, bark-covered paths that wander beside thick plantings of both native and exotic azaleas growing in the light shade of rough-barked loblolly pines (*Pinus taeda*), oaks, tulip trees, dogwoods, magnolias, Japanese maples (*Acer palmatum*), and a few hemlocks. There are other shade-tolerant, mostly evergreen shrubs—rhododendrons, mountain laurels, andromedas, mahonias, fetterbushes (*Leucothoe axillaris*), hollies, viburnums, nandinas, and winter daphnes—but these are planted mainly for variety. There are also patches of vinca, pachysandra, ivy, ajuga, lenten rose (*Helleborus orientalis*), hosta, and daffodils here and there, but most of the ground beneath the shrubs is bare mulch. The stars of this show, in other words, are the azaleas.

They're at their brightest from late March to early April when nearly every shrub is a solid mass of red, pink, white, fuchsia, or purple blossoms. From the observation platform near the parking lot where the trails begin, you can see the woods below, carpeted with bright color.

Like most of the woodland plantings at Callaway, the Azalea Trails are well groomed—the shrubs are fully mulched

Deep red azaleas along the Azalea Trails.

and weed-free, the woods are open and clean, and the paths are smooth. The trails near the observation platform and around Mockingbird Lake, however, are the most beautiful woodland gardens on the site. Here the azaleas get enough light to bloom profusely, and, most importantly, the clusters are large and thick enough to make the garden seem fully and richly planted.

Callaway Gardens was created by the industrialist Cason J. Callaway and his wife, Virginia Hand Callaway. It's now owned and managed by the nonprofit Ida Cason Callaway Foundation, named by the Callaways after Cason Callaway's mother. The Foundation's subsidiary, Callaway Gardens Resort, Inc., operates the stores, lodging, and recreational facilities at the

Gardens, and all its profits go to the Foundation.

One of Callaway's nicest amenities is the Gardens Restaurant, located in the handsome old clubhouse on Mountain Creek Lake. You can enjoy a fine al fresco dinner on the restaurant's long verandah while watching mallard ducks cavort on the lawn by the lake.

The gardens are open daily from 7:00 A.M. to 7:00 P.M. from April 1 through Labor Day; 7:00 A.M. to 6:00 P.M. in March and from after Labor Day through October; and 8:00 A.M. to 4:00 P.M. from November through February. Admission is ten dollars per person or twenty dollars per vehicle (up to nine people) from June through August and $7.50 per person or fifteen dollars per vehicle from September through May.

The gardens are on Route 27 in Pine Mountain, about seventy miles southwest of Atlanta. If you're driving to the gardens from the north, take exit 14 off Interstate 185 and turn left onto Route 27. If you're approaching from the south, take exit 13 off Interstate 185, follow Route 18 to Pine Mountain, and turn south onto Route 27.

For more information, call 1-800-225-5292, or write Callaway Gardens, P.O. Box 2000, Pine Mountain, GA 31822-2000.

Opposite: Drifts of pink and white azaleas carpet the loblolly pine woodlands along the Azalea Trails in Callaway Gardens.

MACLAY STATE GARDENS

The Maclay Gardens, in Tallahassee, Florida, are an easy combination of both formal and naturalistic elements. One of its richest and most beautiful features is the half-mile-long Main Walk that runs from one end of the twenty-eight-acre garden to the other.

The walk begins at the garden entrance and runs through a woodland dominated by massive old live oaks underplanted with magnolias, hollies, dogwoods, and eastern redbuds (*Cercis canadensis*). The walkway is lined with large, dense drifts of evergreen shrubs: mainly azaleas and camellias but also mountain laurel, ardisia, heavenly bamboo, and green-leafed and variegated aucuba. Beneath the shrubs are large carpets of Algerian ivy (*Hedera canariensis*), clumps of cast iron plant (*Aspidistra*), and other low-growing species. The walk is most colorful from early to mid-March, when the azaleas, dogwoods, and redbuds are blooming simultaneously. Although it curves through a woodland garden, it isn't a typical woodland garden path but an elegant, thirteen-foot-wide brick walk, complete with a neat, two-brick-high curbing on each side.

Another charming feature is the well-named Secret Garden, a cool, shady woodland room enclosed by curving walls of tea olive and privet, both grown to tree size. The floor of the Secret Garden is planted with ajuga, heartleaf, selaginella, Chinese

Red azaleas and a white dogwood provide spring color along the elegant Main Walk.

The park is open every day from 8:00 A.M. to sundown. Admission is $3.25 per vehicle (with up to eight people). Additional passengers, pedestrians, cyclists, and other solo visitors are charged one dollar. There's an additional charge to visit the gardens during their peak blooming season, January 1 through April 30. Fees are three dollars for adults, $1.50 for children ages six through eleven; children under six are admitted free.

holly ferns, mahonia, and other plants. Its focal point is a heavy wrought-iron bench and table.

The Maclay Gardens are named after their creator: a wealthy New Yorker named Alfred Barmore Maclay. The house at the end of the main walk, which is open to the public from January through April, was Maclay's winter home from the early 1920s until his death. His family gave the property to the state in 1953.

The gardens are part of a state park that includes a swimming area, picnic shelters, and hiking trails on the shores of Lake Hall.

Thick drifts of variegated Japanese aucuba grow under a massive live oak, draped with Spanish moss, at Maclay Gardens.

The gardens are located just off Thomasville Road in Tallahassee. To reach the gardens from Interstate 10, take exit 30 and drive north on Thomasville Road (Route 60).

For more information, call 904-487-4556, or write Maclay State Gardens, 3540 Thomasville Road, Tallahassee, FL 32308.

BOK TOWER GARDENS

In 1923, Iron Mountain in Lake Wales, Florida, was a sandy hill covered with pines and scrub palmettos. Today, Iron Mountain—at 298 feet, the highest point on the Florida peninsula—is a shady oasis covered with large live oak trees, wide lawns, an impressive, 205-foot-high, neo-Gothic

A long, wide allée of white and pink azaleas under magnolias and Spanish moss-draped oaks at Bok Tower Gardens. Notice the white violas, lower right.

The colors of the orange, white, and fuchsia azaleas are echoed by the red and white impatiens below. Large live oaks stand in the background.

stone-and-marble carillon tower (after which the garden is named), and some of the lushest woodland gardens in America.

The most beautiful woodland vignettes are in the northwest section, along North and Mockingbird walks. Smooth, bark-mulched paths, some as wide as roads, curve gently through an open forest of elegant live oaks. The walks are glorious allées lined with long drifts of azaleas, some of them twelve feet high and as wide as a room. In March, when most of the azaleas are in bloom, the paths are long tunnels of colors—whites, reds, pinks, salmon, and lavender. In addition to the azaleas, there are also camellias, gardenias, dogwoods, and magnolias, as well as viburnums, pittosporums, and other species for variety. An interesting assortment of flowers and evergreen ground covers—including ivy, primulas, violas, impatiens, and mondo grass—decorates the lower layer, and friendly squirrels add even more interest as they scamper about looking for handouts.

The gardens were created by Edward Bok, a Dutch immigrant who made his fortune in publishing. They were designed by

Frederick Law Olmsted, Jr., son of the creator of Central Park, and they flourish on this otherwise relatively dry hilltop because of daily irrigation.

Today the gardens are owned and operated by the nonprofit Bok Tower Gardens Foundation.

The gardens are open every day from 8:00 A.M. to 6:00 P.M. Admission is four dollars for adults, one dollar for children ages five through twelve. (The fees are waived if you enter the gardens between 8:00 and 9:00 on Saturday morning.) Children under five are always admitted free.

A pleasant cafe with an outdoor terrace serves light meals, and the adjoining gift shop has a large selection of garden books and high quality garden goods.

Bok Tower Gardens are near the center of the Florida peninsula. To get there, take Route 60 or Route 27 to Lake Wales and follow the signs to the gardens.

For more information call 941-676-1408, or write Bok Tower Gardens, 1151 Tower Boulevard, Lake Wales, FL 33853-3412.

HODGES GARDENS

Although Hodges Gardens is located on 4,700 acres of mostly pine woodlands in western Louisiana, the majority of its plantings are sun-loving displays of showy perennials and annuals. Many of these flowers are arranged in the treeless bottom of an abandoned quarry that forms a wide semicircle

A statue of St. Francis of Assisi is a focal point at Bok Tower Gardens.

Pink azaleas and red camellias along the elegantly curving stone steps in the pine needle-carpeted woods of Hodges Gardens.

little, bermlike hillocks divide the space into intimate rooms. Attractive concrete paths, their surfaces decorated with small exposed aggregate stones, and elegant stone steps take you in and out of these charming spaces, past clusters of large azaleas and Japanese camellias. In winter and early spring the camellias are decorated with red, pink, and white blossoms. In late March and early April, the azaleas are covered with white, pink, and red flowers. Underneath the shrubs, layers of large loblolly pine needles create an attractive natural mulch.

Hodges Gardens was developed by A.J. Hodges, a wealthy oil producer and lumberman, and his wife, Nona Trigg Hodges, who lived in a house on an island in the garden's manmade lake. Today the gardens are owned and managed by the nonprofit A.J. and Nona Trigg Hodges Foundation.

The gardens are open 8:00 A.M. until sunset every day except New Year's Day, Christmas Day, and Christmas Eve. Admission is $6.50 for adults, $5.50 for seniors, and $3.00 for children ages six to seventeen. Children under six are admitted free.

around the Lookout Tower in the Main Gardens.

The outer edge of this semicircle, however, is shaded by tall loblolly pines, and

Opposite: Pink and white azaleas line a streamlet running through the loblolly pine woodlands.

The gardens are located on Route 171, about twelve miles south of Many (pronounced MAN-e), Louisiana.

For more information, call 1-800-354-3523 or 318-586-3523, or write Hodges Gardens, P.O. Box 900, Many, LA 71449-0900.

DESCANSO GARDENS

If you like camellias, you'll love Descanso Gardens. According to its staff, this Southern California garden has the largest outdoor planting of camellias in the world—more than one hundred thousand plants in all. Most of the shrubs are planted along the wide, smooth paths that curve through a mature, open woodland of

Pink camellia japonicas and California live oaks in the background at Descanso Gardens. (Photo by Don Graf, Descanso Gardens.)

Red and Pink azaleas line a path through the forest of California live oaks. (Photo by Descanso Gardens.)

California live oaks. Nearly all the camellias were set out in the 1940s, so most of them are now the size of small trees. They form tall tunnels of glossy, dark evergreen foliage underneath the gracefully twisting, wide-spreading branches of the century-old oaks.

For accent and variety, the impressive walls of camellias are punctuated by much smaller clusters of azaleas, rhododendrons, variegated aucuba, heavenly bamboo, pittosporum, and other shade-tolerant evergreen shrubs. Some of the twenty-five-acre forest is also carpeted with large drifts of ivy, clusters of clivia, and other plants that thrive in dim light. Most of the ground, however, is covered only with a thick layer of fallen oak leaves, which provide a light brown counterpoint to the deep green foliage of the shrubs.

The oak leaves also make the camellia forest an unusually low-maintenance garden. The slowly decaying leaves create a deep mulch that automatically fertilizes the plantings, retains moisture, and helps keep the garden virtually weed free. Because Descanso gets less than ten inches of rain per year, it's irrigated regularly—but Jim Jackson of the Descanso Guild says even that step might be unnecessary. He speculates that, because the mulch is so deep and the garden so shady—and because it also receives moisture from the fogs that creep in from the Pacific Ocean—the camellias could actually survive on natural precipitation alone!

Pink and white camellia japonicas grow above a thick carpet of ivy and beneath a canopy of California live oaks. (Photo by Descanso Gardens.)

At the edge of the oak-camellia forest is a well-designed Japanese teahouse and a man-made but very natural-looking stream, both of which are artfully woven into the site. The teahouse and its adjacent bridge and decks are all built of dark brown-stained wood that echoes the bark of the surrounding oaks and maples. The graceful bridges, decks, and patios also provide close, bird's-eye views of the stream. The gently flowing brook sounds refreshing as it splashes over tiny waterfalls, and giant one- to two-foot-long carp glide in the still pools between the little cataracts. Along the banks of the stream are lush, ragged drifts of azaleas, camellias, mondo grass, and other plants.

Located in the foothills northeast of Los Angeles, Descanso was the estate of E. Manchester Boddy, editor and publisher of the *Los Angeles Daily News*. Boddy named the property "Rancho del Descanso" (Spanish for "Ranch of Rest"). In addition to planting camellias, Boddy built a twenty-two-room mansion, which is now open to garden visitors, and also planted large collections of roses, lilacs, irises, and other plants. In 1953, Boddy sold the property to the County of Los Angeles, which opened it to the public. Since the late 1950s, the 160-acre garden has been managed by the non-profit Descanso Gardens Guild.

Descanso is open daily, except Christmas, from 9:00 A.M. to 5:00 P.M. Admission is five dollars for adults, three dollars for seniors and students, and one dollar for children ages five through twelve. Children under five are admitted free.

Descanso's Cafe Court restaurant serves sandwiches and light meals, and its gift shop sells plants, books, and other garden-related items.

The garden is located on Descanso Drive in La Canada Flintridge, which is just off the Glendale Freeway (Route 2) and the Foothill Freeway (Interstate 210).

For more information call 818-952-4400 or 818-952-4401, or write Descanso Gardens, 1418 Descanso Drive, La Canada Flintridge, CA 91011.

RHODODENDRON SPECIES BOTANICAL GARDEN

If you think all rhododendrons are medium-to-large shrubs with medium-to-large leaves, a visit to the Rhododendron Species Botanical Garden in Federal Way, Washington, can be a startling experience. You'll quickly learn that the genus also includes two dwarfs (*Rhododendron radicans* and *R. pumilum*) that grow no more than a few inches high and a Himalayan giant (the well-named *R. giganteum*) that reaches one hundred feet. You'll also discover that some rhododendron leaves are only a quarter-inch long while others reach almost three feet.

The garden includes more than 2,100 different varieties of more than 450

The low-growing Rhododendron calostrotum, *in the alpine garden, glows in early morning sun. Japanese stone pines* (Pinus pumila) *grow behind the shrub, and the evergreen forest is in the distance.*

rhododendron species, according to the Rhododendron Species Foundation, the nonprofit organization that maintains the twenty-four-acre garden. According to Scott Gregory Vergara, the Foundation's executive director, the collection includes more than half of the world's known rhododendron species. As the Foundation's literature proudly boasts, the garden is "one of the largest collections of

A large massing of Rhododendron orbiculare. *This pink-blossomed shrub is named for its leaves, which resemble those of sea grapes or miniature waterlily pads.*

species rhododendrons and azaleas in the world."

Unlike many botanical gardens, however, this one isn't another homely outdoor museum of plants. The rhododendrons—many of them more than six feet tall—are gracefully distributed along winding paths in the middle of a classic Pacific Northwest evergreen forest. Giant Douglas firs (*Pseudotsuga menziesii*), western hemlock (*Tsuga heterophylla*), and western red cedar (*Thuja plicata*) provide light shade as well as a dramatic dark green backdrop for the shrubs. Japanese maples, dogwoods, ferns, and other shrubs and perennials add variety. All plants are well groomed and mulched, and the gravel or bark paths are carefully maintained.

Like most of the land along Puget Sound, the garden is in Zone 8. Winters here are like those of the Deep South: mild enough to sustain a large number of rhododendrons

Pale pink Rhododendron Yunnanense, *white* R. rigidum, *and lavender* R. augustinii *at the Rhododendron Species Botanical Garden.*

that would be wiped out in most Northern climates. Thanks to the region's mild, moist climate and the garden's large, diverse collection, at least a few rhododendrons are in bloom here from January to September.

A special feature of the garden is a large, rustic, hexagonal gazebo built at one of the garden's highest points. From its comfortable seats you have a wide view of several acres of trees and shrubs spread out below you.

Just below the gazebo is an alpine garden. Here, tiny, low-growing rhododendrons with boxwood-size leaves (including *R. radicans* and *R. pumilum*) grow among dwarf evergreen trees and large, handsome gray granite rocks resembling an alpine ledge.

The garden is open year-round. From March through May (its most colorful period), it's open daily, except Thursdays, from 10:00 A.M. to 4:00 P.M. From June through February, it's open every day except Thursday and Friday from 11:00 A.M. to 4:00 P.M. Admission is $3.50 for adults, $2.50 for seniors and students. School groups and children under twelve are admitted free.

The garden is on land owned by the Weyerhaeuser Corporation, which also built the garden's greenhouse and several other facilities. The garden is next to Weyerhaeuser headquarters, just off Interstate 5. To reach the garden from Interstate 5, take exit 142A and turn onto Route 18 East; then exit Route 18 immediately and turn left onto Weyerhaeuser Way South. Look for a Weyerhaeuser sign on your left, the first of several that will direct you to the garden.

For more information call 206-661-9377, or write the Rhododendron Species Foundation, P.O. Box 3798, Federal Way, WA 98063-3798.

LAKEWOLD GARDENS

Lakewold is a former estate in Tacoma, Washington, with huge old trees, large lawns, and formal gardens. But it also has three informal areas that teach valuable lessons about woodland garden design.

The most impressive area is the magnificent entrance drive, which was laid out in the early 1960s by noted West Coast landscape architect Thomas Church.

The drive does not approach the residence directly but makes a long circle through a narrow woodland garden on the edge of the property. Like a woodland garden path, the fine gravel drive is bordered by lush, largely evergreen plants: one-hundred-foot-tall Douglas fir trees, mature dogwoods, twenty-foot-high rhododendrons, wide carpets of pachysandra, vinca, and ajuga, as well as bunchberry (*Cornus canadensis*), wild ginger, trillium, cyclamen, and other perennials.

The plantings, and especially the ground covers, are, paradoxically, both lush and restrained at the same time: lush in that they grow thick and full and cover every inch of ground on both sides of the drive but restrained in that there are just a few selections along the entire drive. There's only one selection planted in each space, and most of those spaces are large. The effect of large, lush drifts of just one plant is stunning.

The naturalistic character of the drive is also enhanced by the irregular size and shapes of the ground cover drifts and by the

An eighteen-foot-tall Rhododendron Loderi venus Griffithianum x fortunei *grows in front of a one-hundred-foot Douglas fir to the left of a pink dogwood along Lakewold's entrance drive. Loderi rhododendrons are celebrated for their enormous trusses of fragrant, delicately scalloped white and pink flowers.*

equally irregular placement of the rhodo-dendrons. Some rhodies sweep to the very edge of the driveway, others curve away from it. In the spring, when many of the rhododendrons are in bloom, the evergreen walls of the drive are hung with huge trusses

of pink, white, and lavender flowers. When the loderi rhododendrons (*R. Loderi* var.) are in bloom, the air is perfumed by the exquisite, subtle fragrance of their enormous blossoms.

Another impressive feature at Lakewold is a little stream that cascades down the steep, tree-shaded slope above Gravelly Lake. The stream is actually manmade, but at first glance it looks natural. That's mainly because the selection and arrangement of the stones lining its banks are so artful that the stream looks as if it's always been there—which is about as real as an artificial stream can hope to look. Note how the pipes, the concrete bottoms of the pool—all the obviously *un*natural elements of the brook—are carefully disguised and how only rocks and plants come into view. Note, too, how everything is gracefully irregular— the size and shapes of every rock, the heights and widths of the cascades, the dimensions and configurations of the pools—and how virtually nothing looks artificial or out of place. (The water in the stream, incidentally, is pumped from Gravelly Lake.)

Opposite: Pink and yellow-green Japanese maples, azaleas, and irises line a manmade but natural-looking pool at Lakewold. Notice the tiny waterfall running into the pool. (Photo by Sally Nole.)

Also worth a long look is the Shade Garden on the east lawn, not far from the head of the stream. The garden consists of one enormous tree: a giant Douglas fir, one hundred feet tall and more than two hundred years old; its five-foot-wide trunk and many low, wide-spreading branches make it look like one of those enormous live oaks that dominate the lawns of Southern mansions. The tree single-handedly provides light shade for a large collection of shade-loving plants spread beneath its massive branches: low rhododendrons, azaleas, andromedas, and Japanese maples and graceful drifts of variegated hostas, ajuga, vinca major, aegopodium (goutweed), ferns, trilliums, violets, hellebores, cyclamens, bleeding hearts, candytuft, primulas, and other perennials. The Shade Garden isn't exactly a woodland garden because one tree—even a tree as impressive as this— does not a woodland garden make. But it shows you many of the accent plants that could help furnish a lightly shaded woodland garden room.

In 1987, Mrs. Corydon Wagner donated Lakewold to the Friends of Lakewold, a nonprofit organization that maintains the property today.

From April through September, Lakewold is open Thursday through Monday from 10:00 A.M. to 4:00 P.M. From October through March it's open Monday, Thursday, and Friday from 10:00 A.M. to

3:00 P.M. Admission is six dollars for adults and five dollars for seniors and children under twelve. Guided tours are available from April through September if requested in advance.

Lakewold is located at 12317 Gravelly Lake Drive SW in the Lakewood section of Tacoma. To reach the gardens, take exit 124 off Interstate 5 and follow the signs for Lakewold. The gardens are about a mile from the exit.

For more information call 206-584-3360, or write Lakewold Gardens, P.O. Box 98092, Tacoma, WA 98498-0092.

BLOEDEL RESERVE

Like Lakewold, the Bloedel Reserve is a former estate. Unlike Lakewold, the Reserve is vast—a 150-acre tract of meadows, forests, streams, and ponds at the northern tip of Bainbridge Island, on the west side of Washington's Puget Sound. Most of the woods at the Reserve are nearly wild. Some, however, have been made into beautiful woodland gardens.

The most beautiful are in the Glen, just north of the Visitor Center. To reach the Glen, walk down the steps below the Visitor Center, cross the service road, and

Enormous rhododendrons and pink and lavender azaleas frame the thirty-foot waterfall at the head of the Glen at the Bloedel Reserve.

follow the soft, bark-covered path into the woods.

Almost immediately you'll have a dramatic vista of the thirty-foot waterfall at the head of the Glen, to your left. The cataract creates not one but several shiny cascades as it splashes over moss-covered boulders. Arching over the falls is a thick canopy of large rhododendrons.

The fall looks natural but it's completely manmade, created when a bridge over the brook wore out and a causeway was built across the stream instead. The causeway dammed the brook, making a serene pond on the west side of the road. Rocks and rhododendrons were added to the embankment on the east side of the road, and water from the pond now runs underneath the causeway and plunges down the embankment. So three things—a permanent crossing, a pond, and a rhododendron-shaded waterfall—were all made from just one causeway.

After passing clusters of azaleas and mountain laurels, the path passes under a canopy of western red cedar and heads down the Glen, parallel to the brook. This short path, on the south side of the brook, is the most impressive part of the Glen because the design of its plantings, especially in the lower layer, is clear and simple. The path descends through a mature evergreen forest, between large solid drifts of vinca minor and redwood sorrel (*Oxalis*

A Japanese lantern, bamboo pipe, and bowl surrounded by moss, wild ginger, and ferns in the moist, shady woods near the Japanese Garden.

The large white blossoms of a large Loderi rhododendron create an impressive color display in the Glen.

oregana), smaller clusters of ajuga and Solomon's-seal, and bleeding hearts and other perennials planted for accent. Because vinca is evergreen and ajuga and sorrel are almost evergreen in this mild climate, the path is evergreen-bordered for much of the year. The simplicity of the lower level plantings brings order to the wild-looking woods around them and transforms the forest into a garden.

The path soon returns to the service road, which winds down to a small, man-made pond at the foot of the Glen. The twenty-foot-long pond is surrounded by ferns, primulas, and other moisture- and shade-loving perennials.

After crossing the pond on a handsome wooden bridge, you follow another trail back up the Glen, on the north side of the brook. This path looks wilder than the first. It has fewer evergreen ground covers but more perennials and more evergreen shrubs, including giant rhododendrons, azaleas, Oregon grape, skimmia, Japanese andromeda, as well as columbines, primulas, lily-of-the-valley, and, according to the garden staff, the largest display of hardy cyclamen in the Pacific Northwest. Near the head of the Glen, the path is bordered by huge handsome drifts of the evergreen native wild ginger (*Asarum caudatum*) and dwarf comfrey (*Symphylum grandiflorum*).

Another impressive woodland garden at Bloedel is the short path running through

A red camellia and large, solid drifts of sorrel define the path on the east side of the Reflection Garden.

the damp, mossy forest on the east side of the Reflection Garden. The dark bark path contrasts handsomely with the large, thick, neat green drifts of native redwood sorrel growing beside it. Smaller clusters of ajuga grow beside the northern section of the path and red-flowered Japanese camellias, sarcococca, bleeding hearts, and trilliums add color and interest. Farther away from the path, young hemlocks provide year-round green foliage in the middle layer.

One of the nicest ground covers in the moist forests of the Pacific Northwest is moss. Moss flourishes there, and few other plants evoke the genius of these wet, shady places so well. In the open woods southwest of the Guest House in the Reserve's Japanese Garden, a tiny streamlet creates miniature cascades as it trickles toward the garden pond. The floor of the woodland on both sides of the streamlet is carpeted solely by moss, with just a few other small, herbaceous

perennials for accent. The stark simplicity of the effect is stunning.

The Bloedel Reserve was designed by its former owners, Prentice and Virginia Bloedel, with help from several landscape designers. It's now owned by the Arbor Fund, a nonprofit organization that manages the property according to the Bloedels' wishes.

The Reserve is open daily, except Mondays, Tuesdays, and national holidays, from 10:00 A.M. to 4:00 P.M. Admission is six dollars for adults, and four dollars for seniors and children ages five through twelve. Children under five are admitted free.

Because the Bloedels believed that the Reserve should be crowd-free, no more than two hundred visitors are allowed on the Reserve each day and no more than a few dozen are permitted at any one time. Not surprisingly, it's best to make reservations (by calling TTY 206-842-7631) before you come. Neither pets nor picnicking are allowed.

To reach the Reserve, you can ride the ferry from Seattle to Bainbridge Island, take Route 305 to the northern end of the island, and follow the signs to the Reserve. You can also reach the island from the Kitsap

Opposite: A simple carpet of moss defines a streamlet flowing through the evergreen woods near the Japanese Garden at the Bloedel Reserve.

Peninsula by taking Route 305 over the Agate Pass Bridge.

For more information, call the number above, or write the Bloedel Reserve, 7571 Northeast Dolphin Drive, Bainbridge Island, WA 98110.

OHME GARDENS

Ironically, one of the best designed woodland gardens in America is found in the treeless prairies of Central Washington. The Ohme Family built this garden atop an arid rocky bluff overlooking the junction of the Wenatchee and Columbia Rivers. When they began in 1929, there was nothing there but sagebrush and grass. When they finished more than sixty years later, there were lovely pools and waterfalls shaded by evergreen woodlands with large graceful carpets of vinca, ferns, moss, aegopodium, lily-of-the-valley, and Canadian mayflowers. Thanks to daily watering (by an unobtrusive irrigation system), the gardens are as green as they would be if they were growing on the rainy shores of Puget Sound, one hundred miles to the west.

The heart of the woodland garden is a green sylvan pool set in a deeply shaded private niche and shrouded by western red cedars and other evergreen trees. On one side of the pool is a massive gray ledge. Water trickles down the rock before splashing into the pool in a tiny waterfall. The other sides of the pool are ringed by gray

Water trickling down a ledge and splashing into a green pool in the evergreen woods of the Ohme Gardens.

fieldstones, which are so low that the water almost spills over them, making the pool seem especially fulsome. Surrounding the rocks are vinca, ferns, and moss.

The simple design of this manmade but very natural-looking place is powerful. The deep, shady green forest and the cool water make it feel cool, the splash and ripple of water make it sound cool, and the gray rock and green plants make it look cool. The subdued simplicity of the palette—gray rock, green water, and dark green vegetation—also contribute to the serenity. But while the trees, plants, and rocks are soothing, there is also a wonderful excitement created by the contrast between the splash of the water and the silence of the woods, between the white shine of the falling water and the cool, dark colors all around it, and between the softness of the water and the hard granite rock.

The Ohme Gardens are now owned by the state of Washington and managed by Chelan County.

They're open daily from April 15 to October 15. The hours are 9:00 A.M. to 7:00 P.M. from Memorial Day weekend through Labor Day weekend and 9:00 A.M. to 6:00 P.M. the rest of the season.

Admission is five dollars for adults, three dollars for children seven to seventeen. Children under seven are admitted free but they must be accompanied by adults.

The gardens are just north of Wenatchee, near the junction of Routes 2 and 97. As you approach Wenatchee, you'll start seeing signs directing you to the site.

For more information, call 509-662-5785, or write the gardens at 3327 Ohme Road, Wenatchee, WA 98801.

NITOBE MEMORIAL GARDEN

Part of the University of British Columbia Botanical Garden in Vancouver, Canada, Nitobe is a traditional Japanese stroll garden, built around a long, curving pond. The northern end of the garden, however, is an exciting woodland garden vignette.

Here, under the shade of Japanese maples and massive Douglas firs, a brook plunges over huge rocks on its way to the pond. Like the cascading brook at Lakewold, the waterfall at the Bloedel Reserve, and the pool at the Ohme Gardens, this lively stream is artificial. But, also like the others, it looks natural. In fact, this brook is so well done that it could actually pass for a real one.

The cascades begin high above the path, so high that you can't see that there's no stream above the highest fall, only pipes carrying water back up from the pond. The water then plunges over and between massive boulders that look as if they could have been there forever, but they were actually chosen and erected by Kannosuke Mori, the Japanese landscape architect who built the garden in the late 1950s. As in the cascades at Lakewold, the concrete floor of the brook is carefully hidden by water and stones. The stream also flows naturally, in a gentle S-curve through a little hollow that looks as if the stream had cut it out of the hillside.

Mori's design, however, not only makes the stream look natural. Like the design of the pool at the Ohme Gardens, it also accentuates its most important element: moving water. The banks of the stream are planted sparsely; except for a few trees, shrubs, and moss, there's nothing—no weeds, no fallen branches—to compete with the stream for attention. The shrubs beside the stream—Japanese andromeda, skimmia, and leucothoe—are similar to each other. They all have small, dark, evergreen leaves and

subdued flowers, and in the deep shade of the stream bed they grow a bit sparse and leggy. Unlike brightly flowering shrubs such as rhododendrons, azaleas, and mountain laurel, they don't compete with the water for attention either. In fact, they're so much alike that they don't even compete with each other. However, they do provide contrast: their soft green leaves and delicate branches make the massive rocks look even harder. And the hardness of the rocks makes the water crashing against them look even softer and more fragile—a favorite contrast in Japanese gardens. The delicacy of the water is further emphasized by the rocks placed below the cascades. As the water falls on them, it sounds like the shattering of fine crystal.

Mori helps draw our attention to the largest waterfall in the stream by making it flow over a huge reddish boulder. Because virtually all the other large rocks in and around the stream are gray, the red one is a focal point.

Thanks to artful design, the manmade stream in the Nitobe Garden looks natural. The large rocks are close enough and flat enough to permit strollers to cross the brook easily, but they're not so regular that they look artificial.

Opposite: The waterfall and stream of the Nitobe Garden blend flawlessly into their natural surroundings. Notice how the overhanging upper surface of the tan rock creates the cascade and how the rocks below the cascade make the water splash when it falls on them.

To provide a close, head-on view of the cascades, and to bring us as close to the water as possible, the garden path takes us across the brook. But not on a bridge. A bridge would be too far above the water, it would compete for attention with the stream and, as an obviously manmade structure, it would compromise the wild, natural look of the scene. Instead, we cross the stream on large, flat rocks. By crossing the brook as we might cross it in the wilderness, we not only get close to the water, where we can best savor its noisy ripples, but we also enhance the feeling that we are in a natural, not a manmade woodland.

The garden is open from 10:00 A.M. to 6:00 P.M. daily from March 8 to October 13 and from 10:00 A.M. to 2:30 P.M. Monday through Friday the rest of the year. Admission is $2.50 for adults; $1.75 for seniors and high school and college students; and $1.50 for students in the first through seventh grades. Children under six are admitted free if they're accompanied by adults, as are UBC students and the sick or disabled.

The garden is on Northwest Marine Drive. To reach it from Washington State, take Interstate 5 to the Canadian border, then take Route 99 to Vancouver and turn left on Southwest Marine Drive, which becomes Northwest Marine Drive shortly after the main Botanical Garden.

For more information, call 604-822-9666 or write the University of British Columbia Botanical Garden, 6804 Southwest Marine Drive, Vancouver, B.C., Canada V6T 1Z4.

CRYSTAL SPRINGS RHODODENDRON GARDEN

The Crystal Springs Rhododendron Garden in Portland, Oregon, is a collection of large rhododendrons, azaleas, and other evergreen shrubs in a refreshing natural setting: a lightly wooded island and peninsula on Crystal Springs Lake, where well-fed mallard ducks and Canada geese swim about in its unusually clean spring-fed waters.

Dozens of mature rhododendrons—several of them ninety years old, many taller than you can reach—are arranged along smooth paths that wind through a garden lightly shaded by tall oaks, Douglas firs, and other evergreen trees. A few ferns, trilliums, and other perennials are scattered beneath the shrubs for interest, but the major ground cover is brown bark. Nearly all the plants in the garden are shrubs and trees.

And that works just fine. The rhododendrons are now so big and the groves so dense that they furnish the garden quite nicely all by themselves. The giant shrubs are so captivating that you just don't notice what's underneath them. In fact, the mulch

Opposite: The bright red Rhododendron *'Heart's Delight' makes a stunning contrast with the white* R. *'Loder's White.' Together they create a flower tunnel at the Rhododendron Garden.*

Deep pink blossoms cover a cluster of Rhododendron *'Cynthia.' The treelike, 20-foot-tall shrubs were moved to Crystal Springs Rhododendron Garden in 1950—when they were 40 years old!*

is probably a better ground cover than plants in this garden because the brown bark sets off the shrubs dramatically and helps keep your attention on what are clearly the stars of this show. The bark also enhances the rhodies in other ways: it keeps the soil damper than most plants would (which moisture-loving rhodies appreciate), the decaying bark gives the shrubs moderate nourishment (which light-feeding rhodies also appreciate), and the bark helps keep the garden impeccably groomed—I don't remember seeing a single weed.

The remarkable condition of the garden is a tribute to the members of the Portland Chapter of the American Rhododendron Society and the Friends of Crystal Springs Rhododendron Garden, who painstakingly maintain the garden voluntarily (and who, incidentally, donated many of the rhododendrons in it).

Crystal Springs is open daily from dawn to dusk. From March 1 to Labor Day— when the garden is most colorful—a two-dollar admission fee is charged from 10:00 A.M. to 6:00 P.M. Thursday through Monday (except for children under twelve, who get in free). The money defrays the costs of maintaining and improving the garden.

The garden, owned by the City of Portland, is on Southeast 28th Avenue, one block north of Woodstock Street, and between Reed College and the Eastmoreland Golf Course.

For more information about the garden, call 503-771-8386, or write to Ted Van Veen, garden chairman, at P.O. Box 86424, Portland, OR 97286-0424.

Pale pink Rhododendrons *grow around oaks in* Hendricks Park Rhododendron Garden.

HENDRICKS PARK RHODODENDRON GARDEN

Like Crystal Springs, the Hendricks Park Rhododendron Garden in Eugene, Oregon, is a rhododendron showcase. According to Michael Robert, head gardener, the eight-acre garden has more than 3,500 rhododendrons and azaleas, as well as another 1,500 trees and shrubs. Many of the rhododendrons were donated by members of the Eugene Chapter of the American Rhododendron Society.

Most of the plants are growing under a light canopy of Oregon white oaks (*Quercus garryana*), centuries-old Douglas firs, and other evergreens on the slope of a knoll bounded by Skyline Boulevard, Birch Lane, and Summit Avenue in the eastern part of the city. The shrubs are planted along fine graveled paths that switch gently back and forth, up and down the hillside.

Unlike the rhododendrons at Crystal Springs, the specimens here are complemented by many other plantings: more

The massive Rhododendron 'Mrs. Furnival' *has pink blossoms with dark eyes.* Viburnum cinamonifolium *grows in front.*

A mass of large red, yellow, and white azaleas in Hendricks Park Rhododendron Garden.

than two hundred magnolias; clusters of mountain laurel, Japanese andromeda, sarcococca, viburnum, and other evergreen and deciduous shrubs; large, solid drifts of pachysandra, ajuga, wild strawberry (*Fragaria*), and other ground covers; as well as ferns, variegated hosta, and other perennials and bulbs.

The entire garden is also well groomed—not by volunteers, like the Crystal Springs garden, but by the Eugene Parks Services Division.

White rhododendrons growing amid oaks at Hendricks Park's Rhododendron Garden.

The garden is open daily from dawn to dusk and there's no admission charge. Pets and bicycles are not allowed. To reach the garden, take Franklin Boulevard (Route 99) and turn south onto Walnut Street. Follow Walnut Street to Fairmount Boulevard and turn east onto Summit Avenue. You can enter the garden on either Summit Avenue, Birch Lane, or Skyline Boulevard.

For more information call 504-687-5324, or write Hendricks Park and Municipal Rhododendron Garden, 1800 Skyline Boulevard, Eugene, OR 97403.

RELATED GARDENS OF INTEREST

Several gardens are distinguished by their large and well-maintained collections of shade-tolerant shrubs, perennials, and other plants suitable for woodland gardens. A visit to any of them can help you decide what plants you'd like in your garden.

According to the New England Wild Flower Society, its forty-five-acre botanical garden, The Garden in the Woods, is "New England's premier wildflower showcase." The garden has trees, shrubs, and evergreen ground covers, but it's celebrated most for its large collection of native perennials. For more information call 508-877-7630, Tuesday through Friday, or write The Garden in the Woods, 180 Hemenway Road, Framingham, MA 01701-2699.

Located just a few miles from both Winterthur and Longwood Gardens, Mt. Cuba Center for the Study of Piedmont Flora has a carefully maintained collection of native trees, shrubs, and especially peren-

nial flowers and ground covers. The garden can be seen only by appointment and only on guided tours that are often booked months in advance. For more information call 302-239-4244, or write Mt. Cuba Center, P.O. Box 3570, Greenville, DE 19807-0570.

The Blomquist Garden of Native Plants at the Sarah P. Duke Gardens at Duke University in Durham, North Carolina, is a six-and-a-half-acre collection of trees, shrubs, and perennials. The twenty-acre Asiatic Arboretum currently being planted will feature trees and shrubs from the Far East. For more information call 919-684-5579, or write the Duke Gardens, P.O. Box 90341, Durham, NC 27708-0341.

The Meerkerk Rhododendron Gardens on Whidbey Island in Washington's Puget Sound features a large collection of rhododendrons, azaleas, and spring-blooming bulbs, all displayed in an open woodland of dogwoods, magnolias, and large evergreens. For more information call 360-678-1912 or write the Meerkerk Rhododendron Gardens, P.O. Box 154, Greenbank, WA 98253.

The Miller Garden is a meticulously groomed collection of woodland shrubs and perennials developed by the late Elizabeth Miller at her home in north Seattle on Puget Sound. You can see the garden only by appointment and only on a guided tour. For more information call 206-362-8612 or fax 206-362-4136.

Located only about two miles south of the Nitobe Memorial Garden, the David C. Lam Asian Garden at the University of British Columbia Botanical Garden in Vancouver has a large collection of rhododendrons and other shade-loving plants, all displayed in an evergreen forest. For more information call 604-822-9666, or write the UBC Botanical Garden, 6804 Southwest Marine Drive, Vancouver, BC, Canada V6T 1Z4.

VanDusen Botanical Garden, also in Vancouver, has an immense collection of rhododendrons and other species. For more information call 604-266-7194, or write the VanDusen Botanical Garden, 5251 Oak Street, Vancouver, BC, Canada V6M 4H1.

INDEX

White Room, **25**, **90**, 114–116, **114**, **115**.
Evergreens,
  broadleaved, 64–74, 101, 126.
  groundcovers, 5, 15, 74–76, 136, 149.
  shrubs, xiv, 5, 64–74, 126, 142, 164, 177.
  trees, 12, 19, 167.

F
False lily-of-the-valley. *See Maianthemum canadense*
False Solomon's-seal. *See Smilacina racemosa*
Fatshedera. *See Fatsia japonica* x *Fatshedera lizei*
Fatsia japonica (Aralia japonica, Aralia Sieboldiana), 72.
  'Variegata,' 72.
Fatsia japonica x *Fatshedera lizei*, 72.
Fences, advantages of berms over, 37–40.
Ferns, 4, **43**, 81, 112, **113**, 116, 121, 132, 156, 161, **163**, 164, 167, 168, 172, 177.
Fetterbush. *See Leucothoe axillaris*
Firewood, 18, 19.
Flowers,
  annual, 5, 64, 83, 97, 149.
  perennial, 5, 64, 101, 149, 158.
  See also specific species
Foam flower. *See Tiarella* spp.
Forget-me-not. *See Myosotis sylvatica*
Foxglove. *See Digitalis*
Fragaria, 177.
Fragrant daphne. *See Daphne odora*
Fragrant sarcococca. *See Sarcococca ruscifolia*
Frogs, 56, 58, 97, **106**, 107.
Frost, Robert, xiii.
Fuchsias, 83.
Furniture, 89, 90.
  in Evergreen, 5, 110.

G
Galax urceolata, 76.
Garden in the Woods, The, 179.
Gardenia jasminoides, 73, 149.
  'August Beauty,' 73.
  'Prostrata,' 74.
  'Radicans,' 74.
  'Veitchii,' 74.
Gardening by subtraction, 7–27, **26**, 110, 120.
Gaultheria shallon, 70.
Gazebos, 89–91, 157.
Geese, 136, 172.
Ginger, wild. *See Asarum canadense*
Glacial erratics, 3, 107.

Glen, the (at the Bloedel Reserve), **76**, **162**, **164**.
Glossy abelia. *See Abelia grandiflora*
Gold Dust plant. *See Aucuba japonica* 'Variegata'
Golden star. *See Chrysogonum virginianum*
Goldfish, 56, 58, **59**, 101.
Goutweed. *See Aegopodium podagraria*
Grading. *See Berms; Paths; Ramps*
Groundcovers, 86.
  deciduous, 15.
  evergreen, 5, 15, 74–76, 101, 104, 136, 149.
  See also specific species

H
Hamamelis spp., 3, 4, 22, **26**, 27, 62, 107, 110.
Hamlet, xi.
Hay-scented ferns. *See Dennstaedtia punctilobula*
Heartleaf, 145.
Heavenly bamboo. *See Nandinas*
Hedera canariensis, 145.
Hedera spp., 15, 70, 75, 135, **137**, 142, 149, **153**.
  H. colchica 'Dentato-variegata,' 75.
  H. helix, 72, **128**.
    'Buttercup,' 75.
    'Glacier,' 75.
    'Gold Heart,' 75.
    'Sulphurea,' 75.
Hedges, advantages of berms over, 37–40.
Helleborus niger, 82.
Helleborus orientalis, 142.
Hemerocallis spp., 103.
Hemlocks. *See Tsuga* spp.
Hendricks Park Rhododendron Garden, **82**, 175–178, **175**, **176**, **177**, **178**.
Herbaceous plants, 78–83. *See also* specific species
Herbicides, 14.
Heuchera spp.,
  H. americana, 81.
    'Dale's Selection,' 81.
    'Dale's Strain,' 129.
    'Purple Palace,' 81.
  H. villosa, 129.
Highbush blueberry. *See Vaccinium corymbosum*
Hills of Snow hydrangea. *See Hydrangea aborescens,* 'Grandiflora'
'Hino-Crimson' azalea. *See Azaleas*
Hodges, A.J., 150.
Hodges Gardens, **85**, 149–152, **150**, **151**.
Holly. *See Ilex* spp.

Honeysuckles. *See Lonicera* spp.
Hosta spp., 80, 107, 110, **111**, **113**, **114**, 116, 142, 161, 177.
  'Fanfare,' 80, 109.
  'Piedmont Gold,' 80.
  'Sieboldiana,' 80.
  H. undulata 'Albomarginata,' 80.
Hydrangea spp., 77, 111.
  H. aborescens, 78.
    'Grandiflora,' 78.
  H. macrophylla, 77.
    'Alpenguhlen,' 77.
    'Coerulea,' 77.
    'Compacta,' 77.
    'Niko Blue,' 77.
    'Pink Beauty,' 77.
    'Variegata,' 77.
    H. m. serrata 'Preciosa,' 77.
  H. paniculata, 77.
    H. p. 'Grandiflora,' 78.
  H. quercifolia, 78, 130.
    'Snow Queen,' 78.
    'Snowflake,' 78.

I
Ilex spp., 142, 145.
  I. opaca, 130.
Impatiens spp., **58**, 106, **109**, **110**, 111, **114**, **115**, 148, 149.
  I. capensis, 47, 112, **121**.
  I. wallerana, 83.
Indica azaleas. *See Azaleas, indica*
Iron Mountain, 147.
Ivy. *See Hedera* spp.

J
Jack-in-the-pulpit. *See Arisaema triphyllum*
Japanese andromeda. *See Pieris japonica*
Japanese aralia. *See Fatsia japonica*
Japanese aucuba. *See Aucuba japonica*
Japanese camellia. *See Camellia japonica*
Japanese euonymus. *See Euonymus japonica*
Japanese Garden (at the Bloedel Reserve), **163**, 165, **167**. *See also* Nitobe Memorial Garden
Japanese kerria. *See Kerria japonica*
Japanese maples. *See Acer palmatum*
Japanese pittosporum. *See Pittosporum tobira*
Japanese spurge. *See Pachysandra terminalis*
Japanese stone pines. *See Pinus pumila*
Japanese teahouse (Descanso Gardens), 154.
Jewelweed. *See Impatiens capensis*
Junipers, 102, 103.

113, 119, **126**, 135, 141, 147, 149.
P. mugo, **36**, 102.
P. nigra, 128.
P. pumila, **155**.
P. strobus, xiv, 3, 22, 23, 24, **25**, 27, 37, 104, 107, 109, 115, **116**, 128.
P. taeda, **85**, **142**, **145**, **150**, **151**.
Pittosporum, 73, 149, 152.
'Variegatum,' 73.
'Wheeler's Dwarf,' 73.
Planters, 109, **118**, 119.
Planting, placement, 63, 83–86, 101.
Podophyllum peltatum, 129, 131, 132, 135.
Poison ivy. *See Rhus radicans*
Poison oak. *See Rhus diversiloba*
Polygonatum spp., 4, 135, 164.
P. biflorum, xiv.
P. odoratum 'Variegatum,' 81.
Polystichum acrostichoides, 129.
Ponds, xiv, 4, 27, 49, 56–62, 96, 97, 104–109, **106**, **108**, 164, 167.
Bentonite, 58.
See also Pools
Pools, 3, 4, 49, 56–61, 97, **161**, **168**.
concrete, 58, 161.
fiberglass, 60, 62, 106.
polyethylene, 60, 61.
polyvinylchloride, 60, 61.
Pope, Alexander, 122.
Portland, Oregon, 172, 175.
Primulas, 83, 149, 161, 164.
Priorities, setting (when making a garden), 1.
"Progressive realization," 33.
Pruning, 4, 16–18, **19**, 25–27, **26**, 97, 107, 110.
Pseudotsuga menziesii, 156, 158, **159**, 161, 169, 172, 176.
Puget Sound, gardens near, 156, 162, 167, 179, 180.
Pulmonaria spp., 81.
P. saccharata 'Mrs. Moon,' 81.
'Sissinghurst White,' 81.
Purpleleaf wintercreeper. *See Euonymus fortunei* 'Colorata'

Q
Quercus spp., 3, 14, 129, 131, **142**, **147**, 153, 172, **175**, **178**.
Q. agrifolia, **152**.
Q. garryana, 176.
Q. virginiana, 67, 135, **137**, 141, 145, **146**, 147, **148**, **152**, **153**, 161.

R
Ramps, 29, 34, **35**, 36.
in Evergreen, 36, 37.

Red flower hydrangea. *See Hydrangea macrophylla* 'Alpenguhlen'
Redbud. *See Cercis canadensis*
Redwood sorrel. *See Oxalis oregana*
Reflection Garden (at the Bloedel Reserve), 165.
Rhododendron spp., xiv, 15, **36**, 37, **43**, 58, 65–68, 97, 101, 102, 104, 107, 108, **109**, 110, **111**, **112**, 114–116, 120, 129, 131, 132, **142**, 152, 154, 156, 158, 161, **162**, 163, 164, 170, 172, 175, 176, **178**, 179, 180. *See also* Azaleas
argyrophyllum, **65**.
augustinii, **157**.
austrinum, 130.
calostrotum, **155**.
catawbiense,
'Album,' 67.
'Album Elegans,' 67.
'Cunningham,' 67.
'English Roseum,' 67.
'Everestianum,' 67.
'Nova Zembla,' 67, **78**.
'Roseum Elegans,' **25**, 67, 87, **104**, 120, 122.
giganteum, 154.
impeditum, 67.
loderi, **159**, 161, **164**.
maximum, 67, 86, 107, 109, 110, **114**, 115, **118**, 119, 120, 122, **127**, **128**.
mucronatum cv. 'Magnifica,' 132.
obiculare, **156**.
pumilum, 154, 158.
radicans, 154, 157.
rigidum, **157**.
yunnanense, **157**.
Rhododendron Species Botanical Garden, 65, 154–158, **155**, **156**, **157**.
Rhododendron Species Foundation, 155.
Rhus diversiloba, 15.
Rhus radicans, 15, 22, 24.
Rocks, xiv, 3, 4, 22, 27.
as sculpture, **93**, 105.
in causeways, 53–55, **55**.
in dams, 56–58.
for stream crossings, 50–53, **52**, **171**, 172.
Rooms, outdoor, 83.
in Evergreen, 4, 110–120.
in other gardens, 150.
Rose daphne. *See Daphne cneorum*
Rosebay rhododendrons. *See Rhododendron maximum*
Roseum Elegans rhododendron. *Rhododendron catawbiense*

Rossiter, Scott, 44, 45.
Ruskin, John, 89.

S
Salal. *See Gaultheria shallon*
Sandbags (in dams), 55–58, **57**.
Sarcococca spp., 72, 165, 177.
S. hookerana var. *humilis*, 72, 131.
S. ruscifolia, 72.
Sarcoxie wintercreeper. *See Euonymus fortunei*
Sasanqua camellias. *See Camellia sasanqua*
Sassafras albidum, 3.
Sassafras trees. *See Sassafras albidum*
Screening of views. *See* Views, screening of
Sculpture, 89, 91–93.
in Evergreen, **58**, **90**, 93, 107, **109**, 110, 111, **112**, 115, 116.
in other gardens, **91**, 132, 135, **149**.
Secret Garden (at Maclay Gardens), 145.
Selaginella, 145.
Shade Garden (at Lakewold Gardens), 161.
Sheep laurel. *See Kalmia angustifolia*
Shortia galicifolia, 83.
Shrubs,
deciduous, 15, 64, 77, 78, 177.
evergreen, 15, 64–74, 101, 107, 112, 119, **126**, **142**, 164, 171.
See also individual species
Silverberry. *See Eleagnus pungens*
Skimmia spp., 164, 169.
S. reevesiana, 72.
Smilacina racemosa, 4.
Smith, W. Gary, 129, 130.
Snow trillium. *See Trillium grandiflorum*
Solomon's-seal. *See Polygonatum* spp.
Spanish bluebells. *See Endymion hispanicus*
Spring Garden (at Airlie Gardens), **91**, 136, **137**.
Spruces. *See Picea* spp.
Steps, 35, 36, 37, 120, **124**, **150**.
'Stewartstonian' azalea. *See* Azaleas
Stones. *See* Rocks
Streams, xiv, 3, 4.
enhancing, 49, 50.
in Evergreen, 22, 24, 34, 46, **50**, 97, 112, **120**, **121**.
in other gardens, **150**, 154, 161, 163–165, **167**, 169, 170, **171**.
seasonal, 58.
See also Causeways; Dams; Piers; Rocks; Waterfalls
Subtraction, gardening by. *See*